Are You Ready to Lose Weight?

Charleston, SC
www.PalmettoPublishing.com

Are You Ready to Lose Weight?
Copyright © 2023 by Amanda Lynn Wesley

Hardcover ISBN: 979-8-8229-1888-7
Paperback ISBN: 979-8-8229-1889-4

Are You Ready to Lose Weight?

Having the right mindset for your weight loss goals.

AMANDA LYNN WESLEY

I want to dedicate this book to my friends, and family for the support they gave me while pursuing my weight loss journey and the struggles I endured. I also want to give a special thanks to Oswego 308 Transportation who have cheered me on and also witnessed my transformation. All these people have been there for me through the "thick" and "thin". THANK YOU!

PREFACE

The author of this book has no intentions to manipulate the reader to meet specific criteria or deadlines if the reader chooses to lose weight. The author believes it is up to the reader to decide to take the next step towards a weight loss journey and body transformation. She (author) will also show that losing weight or striving for weight loss success is not only physical but a mental journey to endure. This book will entail strong messages for the reader in order to persevere and succeed on a weight loss journey. No goal is insignificant; striving to reach success is a series of initiatives that lead to the larger picture of an individual's self-victory. The author's goal for drafting this book is to encourage those that are facing weight loss struggles, to not give up hope. Also, the goal is to change the mindset for a healthier lifestyle. She simply wants to *inspire the aspiration* in the weight-loss journey of everyone who may need **added reassurance**. Through her own personal hardships and successes, the author highly values a community of people who showed unconditional support to the author while overcoming personal hardships and succeeded in making a positive lifestyle change. *Losing weight is not only a physical transformation of positivity, losing weight changes the mindset of how someone prioritizes one's outlook on life. The transformation of body and mind are not the end results, but a continuance competency of success for a greater life. Simply put, we are all authors of our own living novels; the pages of tomorrow can be unwritten or prewritten, it depends on the author (YOU) who decides that personal fate. Message from author to reader: Your chapter for a new journey can start today at your own free will! Disclaimer: *Any suggestions that the author makes in this book are based solely on earlier efforts of losing weight and changing life habits which has resulted in both triumphs and failures. The author is NOT a medical physician and does not have a profession in the clinical field of fitness. If you are serious about making drastic changes by weight-loss, please speak to your primary care provider before starting any diet and exercise regiments. Preconditioned health issues, medications, new health issues, and a sedentary lifestyle may play a role in efficiency towards a body transformation. Please keep in mind that the opinions of the author do not reflect the opinions of the publisher.*

TABLE OF CONTENTS

CHAPTER 1

"To improve is to change; to be perfect is to change often."

\- Winston Churchill

THE WORD CHANGE is often looked for as a fear of something new coming, or usually something new that abruptly happens. Change can either be good or bad, depending on how it is reflected in your daily routine. We as humans have seen countless changes in various aspects of our social lives. These changes include the workplace (new management, scheduling, deadlines, etcetera), in a government (new agendas, different political parties governing, etcetera), and even in a school system (new curriculum guidelines, added policies, etcetera). There are many factors in our daily social lives that involve change. Listing what changes in our daily lives can be an endless, well, confusion perhaps? Why can change feel confusing to us, as if we are programmed from day one for how to run our own personal lives? We go to bed knowing what the protocol of our routine is for tomorrow; though, tomorrow comes and that protocol you depend on has vanished. Now what? What would be your "B" if this were to happen? Wait a minute here, do you even have a plan "B"? Hey, there are people who may not have a plan "A"! Amongst this rhetorical question, where does weight-loss come into play in all this? The answer to all of this is, you must figure it out yourself in the game of life. My plan "B" could be different from my neighbor's plan "B" as far as changes go. Your plan "B" is effective to you; however, it differs to your friend. That is one of the many reasons what makes us so unique amongst each other. We can pilot our own plane into the clouds and find where our flight will take us. We can land on a smooth runway or have the choice to pick a runway tucked in between high-peaked mountains that can alter our instruments and cause great risks for landing. Regardless of a smooth flight or a turbulent one, changes are made before, during, and after the trip. Our actions tomorrow are reflected upon the choices we make today. Amongst the flying analogy, you ask yourself again, *where does weight loss come into play in all of this?* I will answer this question from experience that losing weight is both a turbulent and smooth process. Each day is a new day when you are focused on your weight loss goals. Your mind is set, and your body will follow. The neat thing about your body, it can quickly adapt to the fitness regimen that you have committed. The lousy thing about your body is it quickly adapted to the fitness regimen you have committed; so, your efforts and results may vary over time. Your monotonous routine that results in stagnant demeanor is common in the realm of fitness, familiar in everyday life; *plateau* is a cunning villain. Those high-flat hills can be a challenge as hiking on an arid trail in the Arizona desert. You may also feel the discomfort from catching your breath in elevated altitudes while climbing up hills in Boulder, Colorado. Sure, the journey to the top is tough but you managed to see breathtaking views of where you came from. You may have not be able to achieve this victory without fortitude and strength. Pushing geography to the side, according to Merriam-Webster Dictionary, * *"plateau is a period when something does not increase or advance any further."* It also means, *"a relatively stable level, period, or condition."* Let us say you started a diet and exercise routine several weeks or months ago by incorporating light cardio and some weight-strengthening. In addition to exercising, you have been cutting back on carbohydrates and fat intake. Through that time, you noticed your clothes fit looser and the scale in your bathroom shows you dropped a few digits. Congratulations, you achieved your goal! If you are happy to lose a few pounds, then I am pleased to go along with your happiness. If you want to lose more weight and want to achieve the next level of fitness while sticking to the same routine, *hmm... how far will that take you?* You may not see the numbers move on the scale and any added muscle definition in your physique. It is a standstill, what is the solution for this plateau? Change. Do not lose hope but embrace change as part of your fitness journey! The simplest tweaks in your diet and exercise can alter your current situation; the results will come along the way. This program is 2.0 compared to what you originally debuted on. Do not fret, you will peak again and then make some changes once more and thereafter (3.0, 4.0, etcetera)! It sounds like an infinite cycle, right? Oh, it is, enduring an active lifestyle can have its challenges. If losing weight were easy, everyone would all be fitness experts. Unfortunately, our lives move in mysterious patterns, and if you wish to hit milestone goals on your new journey, changes are crucial. The human body needs to be "shocked" regularly before it quickly adapts again. What do you mean the body needs to be "shocked" per say? This book will explain this later. The tips and loopholes of a successful body transformation are an endless bag carrying tangible objects of obstacles, setbacks, growth, and perseverance. With a strong state of mind, you will be resilient to whatever problems life throws at you. I hoped that my analogies highlighted the basic concepts of change and how effective it is whilst earning self-improvement both mentally and physically. This is vital while trying to lose the pounds of excess weight and improving your overall physique. Yet, with strong knowledge and acceptance of change, it is beneficial on your journey. I will discuss how important it is to have a mind-over-matter in the next chapter. I believe in what I am writing because plateaus and changes are what I have experienced in my personal weight loss journey. The lessons that I learned through my journey are one of the reasons I aspire for people to hit their goals effectively. My goal as the author is to make sure you are ready to lose weight and adapt to a new, healthy lifestyle.[1]

---

[1] *"Plateau." Merriam-Webster.com
Dictionary, Merriam-Webster, https://www.merriam-webster.com/dictionary/plateau
Accessed last 5 of Feb. 2022

CHAPTER 2

"To create something exceptional, your mindset must be relentlessly focused on the smallest detail."

\- Giorgio Armani

MIND-OVER-MATTER is a common factor to aim for achievement. It is a widespread belief that when you put your mind into something, you shall achieve what you want. Sounds simple enough; nevertheless, it is a belief that can take a lifetime to grasp. As humans, we are powerful creatures thanks to the brilliant minds that we have. Our minds can dictate our bodies to go somewhere, to move a certain way and to complete tasks. You steer yourself in the direction you want to go, and the body mechanics will follow through. It seems simple and mindless but when someone wants to lose weight or thinks they should be more active, the mind telling the body to go is tougher than one thinks! It may take some reprogramming our minds where taking the initiative, our minds are decided. For the runners out there (like myself) we take the initiative each time we go out on route. Either for training or leisure, there is normally a game plan of what we wear, what to bring, where we are running, and how far we run. With a focused mind, this plan once executed, will have the body go as far until the mind says, *that is enough*. It could be short distance to longer distance. I catch myself out of whim, to go further on a course. At the beginning of my route, my goal was to complete four or five miles and with pure enjoyment and fortitude (or silliness), I will catch myself running over eight to fourteen miles each time! My mind says we are doing this, and the body goes, *okay!* However, my body resents me when listening to my mind, by leaving me feeling sore the next day. I am not here to brag about my fitness level, there are runners and other athletes breaking world records all the time; I feel blessed to share a few similarities amongst these elitists which are persistency, accountability, and willpower. Do you want to know the coolest thing about having these traits in your life? These traits are priceless! Sure, while playing sports, you may have to buy uniforms and costly athletic equipment. For hockey as an example, a player is to be protected in fast-paced periods of the game. A football player needs to be well equipped while being blitzed by a charging opponent. An excellent pair of running shoes can cost a person up to two-hundred dollars or more, let alone taking part in races costs money too (believe me, I know). The bottom line is all the money a person can spend on athletic equipment and apparel will not guarantee becoming a champion. Do YOU believe you can become a champion? You are off to a good start because you began reading this book. This book will provide you with knowledge and ideals that can help you achieve your goals. You are open to learning something new OR need reassurance that you can achieve greatness while on your journey to better health! Please believe me when I say this, most of my youth, I dreamt of being a champion of somewhat though never had a game plan of becoming one. I wanted to lose weight, I wanted to lose weight *so bad*, yet I continued to eat junk food and be sedentary in my old lifestyle. My mind desired greatness but was not ready to follow through. While going through the process of divorce, I announced to myself that this was the time for me to lose weight and take baby steps as I entered a new chapter of my life. I would go for walks and do light exercises at my local gym. I would eat healthy majority of the day and then for dinner, my family would announce, "Let's have Chinese take-out!" *Oh crud!* There goes blowing my healthy diet and exercise. I must say, the entrée of General Tso's must have a secret recipe to make typical, breaded chicken breast transform into a savory glutton of instant satisfaction. I have nothing against this American Chinese dish, it is delicious, but at the beginning of my fitness journey, the food did not help me shred the excess pounds. This humor had enlightened me because I kept myself distracted by pretending to be cocooned in a "healthy atmosphere" while working and being away from home. I packed my own healthy lunches and went to the gym on my way home from work. However, as soon as I walked into my cozy house, I first visited my good friend, the refrigerator! Mentally, I was in a tug of war: my mind had me sailing on the "right" course to weight loss victory; though, the waters were choppy, and I often fell overboard. Thankfully, each day is a new day but making the same mistakes makes you feel you are in the Twilight Zone. I knew I had to change something, or I was not going to see any results. My body was confused as well as my intuition and then one day, my mind became cleared (lightbulb): *I needed to become more disciplined!* I had to somehow train my mind to become laser focused like a bald eagle watching the treacherous waters of a winding river, waiting to swoop down and snatch a large, pink salmon. That salmon meant life or death to the large, winged predator. This felt like me approaching 300lbs which was detrimental to my health and future. What changed me? I had to mentally take charge of my mind and compete to a dynamic level that I did not believe I could perform. It used to be a dreadful walk through the gym doors to see the "gym rats" dead-lifting dumb-bells that weighed about half their size and seeing lean runners sprinting at a pace on the treadmills while their breaths synchronized in a prompt rhythm. *Dang!* I thought to myself. *I do not belong here!* Despite my second guessing I managed to hop on the nearest elliptical machine and focused on my own synchronized breathing. I had to focus on myself, but I did not want to feel too comfortable with my current situation. While watching others at the gym, I quietly competed to reach a level of higher expectation without them knowing that we were competing. After my workout session, I was fatigued but felt I pushed myself better than I have before. *I thought this is what I must do. I cannot keep putting in little effort for exceptional results. I need to focus on what needs to be done and be profoundly serious in my efforts therefore I can achieve my goals.* My mind was slowly adapting to the change that was necessary. I cannot be distracted from what can derail me from my weight loss journey, from my upcoming body transformation. I was ready for a change and my mind will make sure of that. Your mind is the greatest instrument that God has given you. Your mind can calculate plans, manipulate the endeavors to be foreseen and then your body executes without any hesitation. This is your life; this is your journey. If you can see yourself dropping pant sizes or have defined muscle composition, what is stopping you? If you feel stuck and frustrated, it is understandable that your current motives are enabling a stagnant situation. Here is a rhetorical question: what have you done in the last few weeks, months, or even years of your personal fitness journey? Has your past determined the current situation you are in now? If no changes are made, what will the next several weeks, months, or years look like? You can wake up and leave the Twilight Zone, you can change your routine starting at this moment – *scheduling appointments to start a fitness journey is not necessary, walk-ins are available!* Change is needed to alter the current situation, as discussed in the first chapter of the book. The mind only decides that factor to go into play. Holding yourself accountable will help you see tangible results projected from your work efforts. Raise the target high and if you miss that target, you did not fail because you tried anyway. Without attempting is a *real* failure. How can someone know if they are making progress without any accountability and setting ambitious standards? The problem can be solved by being disciplined and taking part in healthy competitions (either with others – secret or no secrets of competing). A group of friends with the same goals can compete; I secretly chose to compete with strangers at the gym, where they are no longer strangers but friends to me now. We must dig deeper into accountability to encourage us to become better achievers. You might be thinking to yourself, a *better achiever? An achiever is an achiever!* Yes, you are correct, achieving large or small goals are all accomplishments. Though, if you strive to hit the largest target that your mind foresees, your minor achievements must lead to greater aims. Raise your level of expectations, and you will be amazed at what your mind can do without any hesitations. Let your mind sail the course to your destination along with accountability to knock the waves behind you.

CHAPTER 3

ACCOUNTABILITY IS A TOUGH PILL to swallow. As an example, a physician may prescribe an ill patient those large, "horse" pills for ingestion to clear an infection (per say). After gulping several of those mini white logs consecutively, the contagion will weaken over a brief time. I do not know many people who enjoy swallowing those pills; therefore, to improve one's health, a sick patient must follow the doctor's orders. Furthermore, if the sick patient skips dosage or does not complete all prescribed medication, the chance of ending the infection is slim to none, *God willingly!* Accountability almost works the same way: to diminish any problems that are distracting you from losing weight, you must hold yourself accountable to stay on track. Holding yourself accountable does not supply any extra opportunity for distractions. If you continue to be resilient and focused on hitting your goals, you will achieve greatness and cut any contagions of doubt and guilt. You "messed up" your diet on a Tuesday because you grabbed a greasy hamburger for lunch, oh well! This does happen but you can make up for the mistake by eating a light dinner to end the day. Feeling guilty is a punishment and discouraging; when you fall off the bike, brush the dirt off your jeans and get back on riding the bike. It includes that life is not perfect and often messy. There are situations beyond our control that have and will sidetrack you momentarily, but at a given time, it is important to restart the journey as soon as possible. This is true IF losing weight and having a healthier lifestyle are both priorities. How many fitness experts or gurus will admit that continuing any fitness journeys may not be top priority? I would say many of them would admit because life includes events that we must address first (family emergencies, moving, job transfers, etcetera.). Life happens with or without you and once the dust settles a bit, if possible, re-establish your priorities and get back on your personal fitness journey. There is a place and a time for everything. It will be okay; I am here cheering you on. That is why I am enthusiastic about sharing my story and what advice I offer in this book! I am an "informal" expert in the fitness realm: my bedroom walls and den are not ornated with degrees and fancy certificates in health and science. I am not a health professional but a person with experience that can relate to those who are struggling to lose weight and want an active lifestyle. I overcame my struggles and I hope my success will shed light for you. You are not alone in this. You can also share your goals with others because they can help you with your journey. At the time of my own journey that I was on, I had a community of supporters who cheered me to the finish line. They saw my great transformation. These people have seen my life change forever because I persevered. I will share later how great it is to have people in awe of what you have endured, and their encouragement has helped you to reach all your goals. There are friends of mine who have lost weight and improved their overall health because they were inspired by my weight loss transformation. Why me as their inspiration? Again, they saw me lose 125lbs in over a year! As the author of this book, I do have the tendency to get off subjects; and with *some apology*, I feel that I have so much to say, and I am trying to make this book compact with personal experience and inspiration without creating inestimable number of pages to write. We went over how life sometimes does not fall in your favor but still be persistent if whenever possible. Holding yourself responsible for your actions will keep you focused on hitting your goals. If you need someone to record your progress, ask that person to hold you accountable. If they say yes, they support you and believe in you. If you missed a workout session or snacked on potato chips late at night, you admit to your supporter and that person will remind you to get back on track. Please try not to feel ashamed from making mistakes, learn from your mistakes and move forward. We are all in this wild fitness jungle together. The journey to a *better you* will be difficult, as it should be. If it were easy to lose fifty pounds, then it would be easier to add fifty pounds or more at any given time. Be strong, embrace the challenges, face defeat with a smirk and push through, all speed ahead! If you are wobbling while walking on a tight rope, wear a harness to keep you from falling. That harness will reassure you that you will make it to your next destination which separates you from where you are currently. Your foot might slip off the rope while you are reaching your next goal. As this happens, you will feel a tug from the harness which will allow you to re-calibrate and continue walking. If both feet slip off completely, the harness is there to hold you in place. That harness is your support and until you climb back on the tight rope, you will be dangling while contemplating taking the next step. That building may be your new lifestyle if you are willing to have it. This is achievable if you enable yourself to continue forward. Taking the initiative and staying focused is what makes accountability a key part to hit all goals. Even though accountability can be a hard pill to swallow, it is effective to beat the negativity and distractions of an invisible infection. Learn to have grand expectations for yourself; you are worthy to become the best person you want to be, and accountability will prove that.

CHAPTER 4

"Failure is the best Teacher."

-Unknown

FAILURE IS A TALENT of mine. What an amazing subject to discuss in this book! I am not being sarcastic, but failure is what brough me here today. If it were not for me to have the woes I had ten years ago, I would not be here today inspiring those who are aspiring. If I were to keep a "front" in my life, who knows what dark place I would end up in now. You can only fake happiness to a point, and I felt with the events that happened to me in the past had me walking on eggshells. How can you enjoy life when you know your world is about to collapse at any given moment? Let us dig deeper into how detrimental the past can be and how it reflects what the future may exploit. Failure is a peculiar subject to talk about and it is emotionally difficult to share. Each of us has come from all diverse backgrounds; nonetheless, we all ride together on the rollercoaster of life. The highs-and-lows in our lives are not constant but it is funny that we often remember the downs more than the ups. We felt a greater impact from the troubles we have endured or currently are enduring. Some issues are hard to suppress, and time can only heal that process. At the end of the day, as humans, we must keep moving to see hope. The other choice of not pursuing further could cost you almost everything. In the early 2010's, I fell in love and three years later, I became a newlywed in June of 2013. During that time, I was a school bus driver while my husband at the time worked side jobs and businesses. It was stressful back then and money was scarce regardless of various sources of income. Trying to manage all these entities and living expenses put a strain on our marriage. Were we too young to wed? It was a possibility, upon other delusional trends that were following suit. We have faced financial troubles, complicated living situations, and other issues amongst each other. To make a long story short, we separated in December of 2013 (yes, six months later we went from "I do's" to "we're done"). Sadly, the separation led to personal troubles as I had to take time off from work because I was not well. The marriage was not as optimistic as I hoped for; though, I managed as much as I could. I also had low self-esteem, maybe *incredibly low*, and settled for what I thought deserved. Throughout my life, I battled with insecurities and inner struggles which brought to depression. I felt that my obesity was the prime factor. My weight bothered me since I was in grade school; constantly ridiculed and bullied. Before entering high school, I managed to lose forty pounds and dropped from a size 16 to a size 9. I went from weighing 180lbs to 143lbs. Here is a side note: after my weight loss journey, I weighed 139lbs but became a size 4 in jeans! Isn't that something? You cannot always go by the scale. The scale does not calculate all the factors that go into play when weighing yourself. Your BMI (Body Mass Index) is the key that figures out more factors than a number on a scale. BMI will be discussed later. As years flowed by while in high school, I successfully regained the forty pounds and managed to gain many, many more! I remembered weighing 210lbs upon graduation. The freedom after high school led to benefits as making any choices you want. I enjoyed the frequent trips to buffets, burger joints, and late-night food runs. At the legal age of twenty-one, greasy pub food was decadent to eat, especially sharing drinks and good laughs with friends. It was all fun and games until gallbladder spasms dampened the party parade. Oh, there were a few trips to the doctor's office and the occasional visits to the local emergency room to treat these nasty spasms! Unfortunately, having the gallbladder removed runs on my dad's side of the family. At the time of this unhealthy lifestyle, I thought I would be next in line to have an organ removed. Going to the doctor's office was often not enjoyable because my physician expressed the need for me to take better care of myself, change my eating habits, and lose weight. She sounded like a broken record to me, but she was right. I did join a gym but was not a frequent flyer. I "tried" dieting yet wasn't serious about changing my eating habits. I would eat only an apple for breakfast, have a light lunch, and then engulf a super burrito for dinner. *Oh, I am rocking this!* Of course not, I had no willpower. I was not disciplined, nor did I want to follow a lifestyle change. I was both dissatisfied and complacent at the time. You know what I am talking about, you could be in the current situation. Facing a faux comfort of complacency and in constant disappointment, it was easier to gripe about problems than to fix them. Unfortunately, in my relationship and marriage, I was more scared and disgusted of my situation. I figured once we separated, there was no hope for me to start my life over on the right foot. On the contrary, it ended up being a blessing in disguise! After my separation from my husband in 2013, I was a basket-case for the next two years between managing the divorce process and personal struggles. Yet, during those difficult years I decided to change my life. I felt I hit rock bottom. I lost many things and moved back home to my parents' home with my tail in between my legs. I felt a total failure, as if I lost everything that I was proud to own. However, what was I proud of owning? While I was married, we struggled to make ends meet. Our opinions and ideas often clashed. The end times were amongst each other. The pit in my stomach stayed with me for the ride. The feeling of hitting rock bottom often feels disgraceful and each day you live in remorse, I know I did. Along with feeling melancholy, how much can a person feel when they are in the pit? How much further can a person dig before they come across bedrock? The digging eventually stops and there is a way to exit out of this situation. You can climb back up to the top! I am not certain how everyone deals with hardships and how they react to their problems, but I do believe we have choices we can make that can bring us back to the surface. While going through my hardships, I noticed something each time I closed my eyes before going to bed. I always imagined two paths that led to places that were completely opposite to each other and the outcomes greatly differed. I would see a fork in the middle of a road, one road led to darkness or emptiness and the other road was hazy, *blurry*, but you can see light in the distance. The path that led to darkness was a flat route, simple, but the end was unknown. I thought that was going to be the path I would take because of the problems I was dealing with; if I were not able to take care of myself, things could be left in the unknown. Quite scary! The other path, the hazy path, that if you were to look at it, you could not quite make out where that path could lead. However, regardless of what the route currently looked like, there is noticeable light at the end of the road. What does that mean? Something easy, like traveling on a flat route but not knowing what the future could look like may possibly be the end of having any happiness. It may start off smoothly and then the path becomes darker as you continue to proceed. Eventually, you cannot see where you are going. Where could this road possibly end? Hopefully, it does not end on a cliff's edge. Or does the path stay dark forever? Is it better to choose the other path? The other road, the one that is hazy and unclear, you draw near it and take a chance to go in that direction. You cannot see too well ahead of you, the path feels bumpy but the sky around you is not dark, *just blurry*. You keep moving, you might have to leap over some large rocks or watch your step between cracks on the road. Eventually, it becomes less hazy and lighter. You start feeling better because you become confident of what possibly lies ahead of you. Then, you noticed the haziness dissipates and the road does eventually end. It led you to a vibrant meadow, and birds fly by and sing aloud because you made it. The sky is clear and rays from the sun force you to squint while you smile in awe of the beauty that surrounds you. Nevertheless, your new surroundings smile back in awe of your journey. A decade ago, my failures were the best of me. I was not quite sure if I would be able to get out of my situation freely or let my woes depict my future. I could take the smooth path of uncertainty and not change my ways or take the path that wasn't clear, but the future remained bright. Looking back, I learned from my failures and chose a direction that was challenging but with risks, came rewards. Great rewards! Luckily, or mostly with motivation, the bumpy road that I trekked was temporary and the future that seemed bright is something that can stay with me for its entirety. This shows that the paths we choose from as our lives are either upside down or right-side up, we follow through what is easy and complacent or uncertain and joyful. Complacency can keep us in our comfort zones and what we do with our time is decided day in and day out. The uncertainty is *growing out* of our comfort zones and dreams that are fulfilled surrounds us. I am not saying there is absolutely no joy when times are bad. There are some good things happening. For me, I still had a job, support, and a roof over my head. But the inner demons made it difficult to embrace what I had. It was until I had to battle with myself first and change my lifestyle until I could truly see my own happiness. I wanted to lose weight; it was not until I was at the fork of the road that I finally made the decision; that was the time for me to do it. I was ready for a change; I chose the uncertain road, and my ambition led me to the meadow. The meadow of newfound happiness and beauty. It was something I had been longing to look for and finally made it happen. Have your story begin today. Close your eyes and imagine what your life can look like a year from now: you successfully hit your weight loss goals, you are feeling healthy, and appear to be a brand-new person. Are you dreaming that? This dream can come true if you decide today to embark on the rough path to a meadow of vibrance. Your decisions today will be seen in the future! You can control the pace of how soon you want to get there. This is your life; you can mold it into something as vibrant as you truly are! It is true that storms come in and go in our lives, if you can endure one storm, the next one coming in might be easier to manage. Do not be afraid and choose the road that will get you to your destiny.

CHAPTER 5

TO MOVE FORWARD is a constant struggle when you feel you keep moving backward. In 2014, I was overwhelmed with the divorce process and getting my life back on track. Each day felt like a nightmare, yet with the feeling of hope and staying persistent I kept going. Trying to focus on my health gave me some distraction while the proceedings continued. I had a yearly checkup with my doctor in April of that year. Sitting in the waiting room, I already imagined what my doctor would say to me this time: *You are twenty-six years old; you need to eat better and be more active, you need to lose weight. I am worried about your health!* "AMANDA!" I snapped out of my thoughts and followed the medical assistant into the room. At the time, the worse thing is about to happen, getting on the scale. I approached the scale and kept my eyes closed until the medical assistant said, "Okay, you can step off..." I looked at the scale and I weighed 264lbs. Gasp! At my office visit, I remembered some things that my physician said but what I recalled the most was that number on the scale. That number frightened me. I knew I gained weight, and it seemed I average twenty extra pounds per year seeing the doctor (it shows how often I weighed myself at home which was a rarity). Although, 264lbs was the tipping point for me. It showed me that I was thirty-six pounds away to weigh an even 300lbs. *I could not let this happen to me; it will not happen!* I finally snapped. I can recall the next day after my doctor's appointment, I started to embark on my weight loss journey. This was it; it begins now. When I first started, every day I ran five miles in the morning, lifted weights at night and my calorie intake goal was 300 calories. Did you believe the last sentence? I was totally joking! I was nowhere near to have that crazy ambition in the beginning of my journey. Also, you would need to consume more than 300 calories if you are going to run five miles each day and lift weights at night. *I know this.* On the contrary, I started the next day by going on a thirty-minute walk in my neighborhood. I did this at least three times a week. After my walks, I lifted my lightweights at home and watched my diet. It was a start, nothing extreme. It was nothing out of the ordinary, I believe anyone can go for a walk and lift 5lb dumbbells for several reps. I called this stage of the journey, **baby steps stage**. If someone were to jump all into an extreme workout regime and crazy dieting, how long would that journey last? The moment a person gets injured or blows the diet, discouragement hovers over their head and the journey is over. If the initiative of the weight loss journey were taken as baby steps, the person would have a chance to continue another day, focused on completing goals. Before summer hit, I gave in and joined the local gym because I was becoming bored of my current routine and wanted access to some exercise equipment. While increasing my activity more, I changed my diet less. Earlier in the book, I mentioned that I made better food choices throughout the morning and day, however my diet plan faltered in the evening for dinner. I still made these mistakes in the beginning of my journey. After a month of seeing little results from my workout routines, I learned that I was wasting my time and energy exercising because my eating habits were still poor. My mind changed and moving forward I jumped into a better diet plan that would help me overall and keep me on the right track to hit my goals. My biggest dream was to lose at the most 140lbs, and I would settle to lose 125lbs! That dream was very intimidating because losing that much weight will take hard work and discipline. I needed to be my own drill sergeant and stay in boot camp longer than any other cadets. Just think, losing a hundred pounds is daunting, *let alone losing at least twenty-five more!* I had my work cut-out for me. I thought about doing the gastric sleeve and lap-band surgeries, but I had this little, annoying bird telling me I can achieve this dream on my own. In my heart, I could see this dream come true for me; but my mind said, *will this dream come true?* It can come true if I become disciplined and persistent. I picked the road that is hazy and uncertain to travel. Yet, I know the breathtaking scenery is waiting for me to get there. This pattern of commitment and determination was not an overnight success. Each day was a step closer, falling into the rhythm of a new lifestyle that I did not see myself having until I reached my final goal. The funny thing is I figured I would lose enough weight, even if I lost 100lbs, that I can resume back to my old habits and "enjoy" the life I knew. That life I knew fell into my old comfort zone. I said I wanted to go back because losing weight has currently taken me out of a comfortable zone into an *uncomfortable* zone. I had to remember: if I improve myself, the uncomfortable because comfortable. Growth leads to greater opportunities. Once you finish this book, I ask you to simply learn one thing out of this reading: **once you complete your weight loss journey, you cannot go back to your old ways of eating poorly and not exercising**. IT IS A LIFESTYLE CHANGE. If you dreamt of becoming fit and healthy, you must remain fit and healthy. It is a new lifestyle that you need to adapt. THERE IS NO GOING BACK. Okay, you could go back, but the challenging work that you have done will go away. Please, do yourself a favor and be serious that this is what you wanted. *This has always been what you wanted*. Adapt to the new lifestyle and do not look back. When I wrote this chapter, I chuckled to myself: the change in me was happening during the worst times, it was not at the finish line of this marathon race. Wow, how amazing human beings are. We can adapt and grow in the worst situations and bloom into beautiful roses. I heard of an old saying that we are not only human beings but human *"be-comings"*. If we are in control, we can become what we want to be and have happiness follow us along the way to greatness! God gave us free will and we are free to make our lives worth something. Although, every step taken you may have to take three steps back. Progression is sometimes followed by regression. I discovered a predicament *(oh, one of many I suppose)* in the beginning of my fitness trek. There will always be a conflict: someone must throw a wrench in between your motors. Why? Like we discussed in the beginning of this book, life works in mysterious ways. We are not always on Cloud Nine nor we are in the bottom of a deep bucket. Life can also be a rollercoaster: the ride takes us high into the sky and then we experience zero gravity as we zoom down fast. It is difficult to get off the ride while it is in motion; we must stick to it the whole duration until we can safely exit out of the car. In other words, we must manage whatever life takes us, and do our best to resolve any problems along the way.

CHAPTER 6

"The way I see it, if you want the rainbow, you gotta put up with the rain."

-Dolly Parton

OUR BODY WILL COMMUNICATE to us in peculiar ways; instead of focusing on what verbal things come out of our mouths, we should silence ourselves and listen to what our bodies try to tell us. I am going to share my personal story on how this all relates. When I was a young girl, my hormones were abnormal. At eleven years old, I received my first menstrual cycle in May of 1999. No big deal, right? Sure, it was important for a girl to receive her first period, but the next cycle did not happen until August, the first day of 6th grade. My periods were not always regular, on the contrary it was the norm for me to skip every other month. I envied those who can write in a calendar when exactly their menstruation cycle begins each month. Shoot, I was lucky enough to receive a period even if it lasted three days! After my childhood and teenage years, I still had issues of menstrual irregularities and hormonal imbalance. I had to do routine blood work to check some of the abnormalities in my blood panel. I have had a few pelvic ultrasounds that found follicles on my ovaries and a cyst on one of them (quite common). Unfortunately, those follicles cause headaches for the reproductive system and alter menstruation. After a pelvic ultrasound in 2012, I was diagnosed with Polycystic ovary syndrome (PCOS). At the time, I was not familiar with this disorder but was told it can be treated. According to Mayo-Clinic.org, *Polycystic ovary syndrome (PCOS) is a hormonal disorder common among women of reproductive age. This disorder causes infrequent or prolonged periods and may have excess of androgen levels (male hormones). Ovaries may develop numerous small collections of fluid (follicles) and fail to regularly release eggs.* I am not going into further detail on signs and symptoms because there are many; the key part of PCOS is that signs and symptoms are typically more severe if you are obese! After doing my own research on this disorder, I felt like my life was over. I dealt with acne in my youth and as a young adult (excess levels of androgen levels). PCOS disrupts the metabolism of the body, depression, anxiety, eating disorders, and infertility to name a few complications from this heinous disease! Oh, and what caught my eye from the research is that having PCOS makes it exceedingly difficult to LOSE WEIGHT. Why would this disorder make it difficult to lose weight? Let me elaborate on this: insulin plays a significant role in our endocrine system. Insulin also affects our hormonal levels. Mayo-Clinic.org explains that *"excess insulin is the hormone produced in the pancreas that allows cells to use sugar.*

[Our energy supply] If your cells become resistant to the action of insulin, then your blood sugar levels can rise, and your body might produce more insulin. Excess insulin might increase androgen production, causing difficulty with ovulation. "This also explains why I was pre-diabetic at the time because my body produced too much insulin (poor eating habits affected this too). White blood cells are affected by PCOS, and the WBC count is typically reduced which is shown during my routine blood work (my WBC count is still lower than considered normal range). Unfortunately, there is no magic medicine out there to cure PCOS. There are many medications and treatments that help women with this disorder which can reduce symptoms and increase chances of fertility. PCOS can cause I begin to see my physician routinely about some treatments for this disorder. At one of my appointments, she prescribed me to take birth control to help treat my symptoms. The birth control gave me monstrous mood swings and I ended up with an allergic reaction to the brand of birth control that I was on. I was not satisfied with the treatment, and I asked my doctor if there is another way to treat PCOS. She tried another method of treatment and prescribed me metformin. Many people think metformin is only used for treatment of type 2 diabetes. It is also used in the treatment of PCOS. The Mayo-Clinic website explains that *"[metformin] improves insulin resistance and lowers insulin levels."* There are other medications that the physician can prescribe for fertility (Clomiphene as an example), but metformin can also aid for greater chances of pregnancy. For those who are pre-diabetic, the website states that *"metformin can also slow the progression to type 2 diabetes and help with weight loss."* I have taken metformin in my early

20's to help regulate menstrual cycles and the possibility to lose weight. Except on my end, I was not compliant being on a drug regimen. Therefore, I did not experience the positive effects from the medication, so I gave up taking it. When I was reapproached to metformin the second time in 2014, I decided to be disciplined and take it faithfully daily. I would say after three months of taking the medication, there were positive changes happening to my body. My periods were regular, and I saw better results in the effort to lose weight. Would I encourage women who are struggling PCOS to take metformin to help them lose weight? It is a maybe and a maybe not. My body reacted positively to taking the medication while Miss Sally Sue could be having terrible reactions from the drug. Our own chemical compounds slightly differ from each other. If you are curious about taking metformin and have been diagnosed with PCOS, I highly recommend you ask your physician to inquire more information. There are many drugs and treatment plans that are now available to treat PCOS, but each plan may not work with everyone. Like any other medication out there, metformin has side effects too. Although, on the Mayo-Clinic website, the article has said that changes of lifestyle are highly essential regardless of what "super drug" is out there to combat weight loss. Can you figure what changes these may be? Here is a hint, regardless of who is diagnosed with PCOS or not, it is right for everyone: diet and exercise. The article explains that *"Maintaining a healthy weight can reduce insulin and androgen levels and may restore ovulation."* The website also suggested to be on a *"low-carbohydrate diet and to incorporate complex carbohydrates."* (Complex carbs and simple carbs will be discussed later in this book). Oh, and my favorite one that the website advised is to be active and exercise routinely. These are good remedies to follow but once again, ask your physician if you believe you may have PCOS (therefore medical testing can be ordered), if you do have PCOS, ask your provider what the best plan will be for you (not for Miss Sally Sue). Your provider may have treatments for you to follow that are proper for your health and needs. In conclusion of all this medical jargon (I also feel this is a drug commercial), I started to see faster weight loss results from diet and exercise, especially with my hormonal levels being adequately normal. If you have PCOS or a disorder that impairs you on your weight loss journey, please do not let it discourage you from reaching your goals. Do your research, see your physician (if you do not have one, get one!), weigh out your options (no pun intended), and take it from there. I am not a medical professional, but please do what is best for your health and wellbeing. Your journey will have setbacks and obstacles along the way to your destination. Ask questions, get answers, start the plan, and remember to not be discouraged because having faith in what you can control will keep you moving ahead![2]

---

[2] *"PCOS". Mayoclinic.org
Mayo-Clinic
http//www.mayoclinic.org/diseases-conditions/pcos/symptoms-causes/syc-20353439
Access last 13 of Feb. 2022

CHAPTER 7

-Unknown

MISERY THAT LOVES COMPANY will have a small group of followers because at some point, misery will remove company itself. It is often that we preach to others and remind ourselves that life is not fair (or works mysteriously-*you got the hint!*), meaning there is an imbalance of events that are either cruel or sweet. *The rollercoaster of life will always have passengers.* Hey! Did you read that last sentence verbally? *The rollercoaster of life will always have PASSENGERS.* This has been mentioned previously, we are often the passengers engulfed in the uncertainty of events in our lives. Whether we are on a rocket ship heading to space or on a ship sinking to the bottom of the ocean's floor. There is more than one person in this world going through scenarios. Meanwhile, you

32

may be *shooting* to the stars, and have a friend or family member on a boat submerging in water-*vice versa*. Nevertheless, we all go through events in our lives. These events may be both terrifying and terrific, now that is a catch-22! What I am explaining is your shadow is not the only object watching your actions from behind. We as humans are great observers; though it leaves room for debate about who is attentive. Even oblivious people may see differences in daily routine by an event altering their general perspective. *Any good deed is left unnoticed*-we have all heard that before! Now what if that good deed is a deed that you give to yourself; do people notice that too? Absolutely they do, especially at a personal level of a relationship. Besides your shadow following nearby watching you on your fitness journey, there are individuals noticing your actions and are astonished. Congratulations, you have a live audience watching a series of segments of your weight loss series and expect a phenomenal season finale! Also, people will notice a glow and bright aura when you enter a room, because a bright smile is attractive! Yet, people can sense someone who is troublesome by seeing a gloomy face that is suffering from anxiety, stress, and depression. These warning signs are truly a cry for help, even if you are not asking for help. In late spring of 2014, I was working diligently in my weight loss regimen and working full time. I was a school bus driver at the time; therefore, I would see my coworkers every day during the school year including in the summer because there are students who attend summer programs and bus transportation is needed for that purpose. For that reason, it is possible for a bus driver to work year-round and like I said, I usually see my coworkers every day. Just like you at your employer, you see your coworkers day in and day out. In the Present Day, I work currently for a large medical group. My current coworkers, and I would jokingly tell each other each morning, "Welcome Home!" Do you know that feeling? The weekends go so quickly, you thought you were on a long lunch break and then it is back to work. I know most of us can relate to that. The point is that your coworkers become family from all the time you spend at your job. I am not forcing anyone to become best friends with their colleagues, but it is ideal to be tolerable and have a positive work relationship with each other. Thus, the workload gets done more effectively, without any real drama. This exceptional group of people usually know what some of their peers are going through in their personal lives. I am sure you have some fellow coworkers that you talked to all the time about home life and other events going on socially. I also believe that you may have a colleague who can turn to you for whatever advice that person needs to hear. Sometimes these people become best friends, regardless of whether one of them leaves the job or not. The bond of strong friendship between employees, your fellow comrades, is something to cherish and appreciate. At the end of the day (and workday), your coworker can fall into your inner circle of friends. While bus driving, my coworkers saw me at my worst and knew I was suffering in my personal affairs. I stayed mostly at the bus barn (or transportation hub) throughout the day. I had a long commute to work because I moved back home. Meanwhile, I would talk about what was happening with my coworkers because I needed constant reassurance that my problems would eventually be resolved. They were kind, understanding, sympathetic, and encouraged me to push through each day. I am delighted to say my coworkers were there for me at my deepest low. Even to this day, I still communicate with them regardless of me moving on and working in a different field of employment. Now let us talk about family. You may have a large, blended family or a small, tight knit family. You may have relatives who live a few houses over or relatives that are a few states away, or in another country! Despite the size and distance, home is where the heart is and family is the heartbeat that keeps you going, *that keeps you alive*. My entire family, especially my parents, were my heroes while going through the turmoil of a failed marital life and inner woes. The unconditional love, support, and lecturing has helped me fight another day. Being lectured by parents does not always involve eye rolling from the peanut gallery; in fact, parents simply want what is best for their children. My dad always told me, *"The most expensive school is the school of life, and you're never gonna graduate it from it."* I think of this quote daily. Oh, and how can I forget another group of people in your inner circle-your friends! You sometimes compare your friends like family. You may tell them more personal things than your own kin. Those who may not have a large family or lost communication with them turn to their friends for love and support. Friends do come and go; however, the ones that are there for you through the thick and thin, their friendship is more valuable than any designer purse. Their outreach to you is priceless. I know someone who is reading all this is thinking, *well I live alone or work remotely, how am I going to receive care and love from other people?* One person knows at least one other person, how did you come into this world in the first place? Pets are great companions and show unconditional love when you feel the world hates you. But pets aren't ideal communicators when asking for advice and guidance. If you are battling serious issues or in a horrific situation, please seek help. Do not feel ashamed or afraid, you will feel okay from the outreach of others. There are people who work in a profession to help those in serious trouble. They pour out their love and empathy because they are committed to helping you get better. Love and support may be invisible to the naked eye, but these feelings are tangible, and we feel it in our hearts. *The power of love can truly make the world a better place.* The irony in all this is that I wrote this chapter on Valentine's Day. You might be thinking to yourself, *here she goes again side tracking and not talking about weight loss goals.* Though, if you are not mentally fit, how are you able to complete a commitment to lose weight when the struggle to live daily is overwhelming? There is an intervention needed to change the mentality and attitude of one's mind. If you are in this situation, seek outreach from someone and ask for guidance. Embarking on a journey to a healthy lifestyle involves not only our bodies transforming into something great but as well as our state of mind. The rollercoaster of life is never vacant for passengers; we are all in this crazy world together. For that reason, let us help each other push through obstacles, and strive for a life filled with good health and prosperity.

**If you have suicidal thoughts or know someone who is suicidal, please seek professional help at once. The National Suicide Prevention Lifeline is available. Please contact 1-800-273-8255 or visit http://www.suicidepreventionlifeline.org for more information.*

CHAPTER 8

"The secret of change is to focus all of your energy not on fighting the old, but on building the new."

-Socrates

LIFE IS FULL OF DO-OVERS. When we are in the pit of woes, it gives us an opportunity to climb up and see how blue the sky really is. Once we are out of a hole and standing in a scenic field of vibrance, we see the horizon of opportunity that can lead us to our own pursuit of happiness. We breathe in the opportunity and exhale with optimism. The expedition to greatness does not start until the first foot moves forward with the second foot following. I discussed my personal life in the last few chapters. Quite frankly, that was emotionally exhausting to share because the scars are there, faded but there. I wanted to feel real with you as the author and that we can all relate to the hurdles we have in our lives. I felt improvement in my state of mind thanks to the reassurance from my inner circle. My weight loss journey became an actual expedition while still managing my hardships. Having a clearer state of mind makes it easier for better decision making and doing things in *any given situation*. Ah, now let's reflect on what we have talked about thus far. In the beginning of the book, we talked about change and adaptation. Also, being mentally prepared for whatever we decide to do. We embraced accountability and accepting our actions. Enduring personal life of hardships and the failures we can learn from. We went over health disruptions and embraced the power of love and support from an inner circle. That is intense in this book. Is this book about losing weight or finding your true self? It is mixture of both, these two subjects are like two peas in a pod. I thought I would find my true self after my weight loss transformation while looking back, my true self was unraveling throughout the process. Let's compare ourselves unraveling like a simple fruit. Take a banana for instance. You grab a banana and start peeling it; the first skin peeled off you see some of the edible fruit. Then you peel the next flap of skin; that skin may have some brown speckles on it, but you continue to peel the entire fruit. You can smell the ripeness from the banana being bare, it is in great shape for consumption. Sure, there could be some bruising on the banana, but it does not alter the taste as much. Am I calling you a banana? *Uh-not necessarily*, but if you think this analogy is strange, I give you the right to call me a banana. *Amanda the banana*, hey it rhymes! As I was peeling off the negativity in my life by losing weight and changing my mindset, I noticed the real me, a vibrant me, through the parts that were peeled. As I reached my final goal, I was elated about who I became. Yes, I mentally pictured some bruising from the past but that did not stop me from becoming ripe and able to consume a better life. *Please do not eat me.* See, I mentioned about health in this book, I used a banana as an example! All light humor to the side, when we adapt to change, it gives us the power to generate the possibility of achievement. We must remove some layers to see the vibrance in us (noticed that I love the word **vibrant**). That is an achievement because we have these hidden talents that can mold our lives into whatever we want! Hmm, are we real *shapeshifters?* I know I am, my body shifted from weighing almost 300lbs and became less than half the size! *I was one, hefty banana to peel.* Are you ready to *shift your shape?* I smiled while asking this question because if you are mentally prepared to change then you are ready to be committed to one of the most exciting journeys in your lifetime! The journey will be hard, and you must stay focused to keep your eye on the big prize. Do you believe you can work hard and be focused? It is possible if you believe that you can. I can say that you are ready to begin the weight loss journey but if you tell yourself that you are ready, then you are truly prepared to start the first step. Let us make this happen, you have enlightened yourself this far while reading this book. It all begins with this simple question: Are you ready to lose weight?

YOUR WEIGHT LOSS JOURNEY BEGINS

CHAPTER 9

"Success isn't overnight. It is when every day you get a little better than the day before. It all adds up."

-Dwayne Johnson

TO START SOMETHING NEW is to leave behind something old. I am going to explain the importance of getting actual results from diet and exercise. The first step is to start a good habit. There have been studies conducted that it takes **21 days** to form a habit. This is the amount of time to form a good habit; it shows, what we want to improve in our lives takes time and dedication. To form a bad habit, it probably takes less time than that. Every person on this planet has both good and unpleasant habits in their lives. People with good habits show traits of punctuality at the work-place, are dependable, and hardworking. These people can also have a habit of being immaculate and health conscious. A good habit can also be a form of saving money, paying off debts, and be-ing frugal. These good habits, to name several, have produced **positive results**. Now we can create a list of the unhealthy habits people have! No, not really, what has been previously mentioned about good habits, we can imagine the opposite. Therefore, why waste our time creating a list of unpleasant habits? I will use a cou-ple of unpleasant habits in a story to share. This story is something we can all relate to because it could be happening right now to someone. Prior to fulfilling my weight loss journey, I had a habit of ordering out too much and making poor food choices. I was too lazy to turn on the oven to bake and I was too impatient to wait for food to be baked. How simple it was to make a phone call for deliv-ery and takeout. I also was not a motivated person and by motiva-tion, I lacked the drive to hit my goals. I can recall going for occasional walks but was not serious enough to stay consistent. I was lazy and spent most of my free time watching T.V. or playing games on my computer. I would constantly play *The Sims* game series and loved watching the characters I created succeed in their "made up" lives but was not motivated to succeed in something of my own. These habits continued while I was married. The sense of complacency and comfort kept me somewhat happy. It was not until the rug was pulled underneath me that I had to amend myself for a better life. Consider the turmoil a blessing in disguise, everything happens for a reason, right? In the last chapter, I mentioned in the beginning of my journey that I went for walks and did light-weight exercises. I then joined the gym to have more workout opportunities. The gym clearly helped me with this factor because the rest became history. Also, I was taking baby steps on how this whole-weight-loss-journey-thing worked. It was uncertain and out of my comfort level, yet creating a habit of this change eventually brought me comfort again—*new comfort*. Both my mind and body adapted, and that was great! I also followed a habit of taking my medication (metformin) to regulate my hormone levels. You would think that things were going spectacularly; no more changes must be made, and I created the only habits that I needed to lose weight for good! Not completely so! I lost ten pounds in a matter of three months and that was because I stuck to the same routine and did not completely change my eating habits. It was recent for me to be medicated but regardless, I hit plateaus. *The definition of insanity is doing the same thing over-and-over again and expecting different results!* The first step to weight loss is creating a good habit but we must take it further than that. You must break barriers if you want to see growth. Growth will lead to results. The first barrier you come across will alter your growth thus will not see any more results. These barriers, or plateaus, are part of your fitness trek. You can create a great habit by creating good habits along the way. If this is not quite clear to you, let me explain. Do you recall in the beginning of the book that the dictionary's definition of a plateau is a subject of something flat and stays constant? If your current weight loss seems flat and constant, you are not alone. You have proven the first habit of becoming active and eating healthier is beneficial and will help reach your goals. The next task is to make sure you have creativity in your new habit to continuously get results. If you say that there will be changes in your new habit, then you are correct. These changes are simply **tweaks** to a system that is already proven to be effective amongst those who have lost weight and **support healthy weight management**. These tweaks consist of changing your workout routine and healthy eating habits. When you begin your weight loss journey, what is your first plan of an exercise regimen? Do you see yourself going on an elliptical daily or take walks at a local park? Do you spare free weights at home and do strengthening in your office or den? Do you practice thirty second planks during commercial ads on television? Maybe you like to jam to your favorite music and dance when nobody is watching! Truthfully, these sound like great ideas to begin a journey; I would love to join you! The start of your weight loss trek may feel odd, but you manage to make it fun. It should be fun, and it becomes exciting when you put in the effort and see the numbers on your bathroom scale move *back*. This excitement keeps you motivated to repeat the routine again, and again, and again... This pace is like healthy eating habits; yes, even eating the exact same healthy food repeatedly can come to a slow halt and you are faced against a plateau (one of many to come). In the early days of me going to the gym (around 2014-2015) the gym owner at the time gave me great advice while I struggled to lose more weight. He suggested that I should sporadically "shock" my body in my regime therefore it won't quickly adapt to a new physical activity. It is like you are throwing a surprise party for the same friend who is already annoyed with you from throwing recent surprise parties in the past. Mix up your exercise routine and diet, continue to have fun and most importantly, *keep challenging yourself.* If you run out of ideas of what to do next, there's resources available to incorporate in your weight loss plan. Examples for innovative ideas consist of *but not limited to* fitness books/journals, online videos, social media, picking the brains of local fitness enthusiasts, personal trainers, and etcetera. These plateaus happen to the best of us. Therefore, it is ideal to often think outside of the box. Staying inside a box becomes small for someone who continues to grow. If you think inside the box, your beliefs will limit your decisions to succeed. A goldfish that stays in a five-gallon tank may stay small in stature. You put the same fish in a larger aquarium, it will become big and have more room to swim. As you make these changes in your fitness routine, there is a key element to be aware of: diet, decisions, and habits. During my journey, exercising was "easier" than watching what I ate. I am not a dietitian but based on experience, a good diet plays a bigger role than exercising alone. Not only does it matter what you eat; it also matters how much you eat. **Rationalizing** your food portions has multiple benefits. Rationalizing food portions can help reduce cholesterol and sugar levels. *Here is a secret:* If you make a dinner plate consisting of grilled chicken breast, cooked broccoli, and a plain baked potato, eat the vegetable first, then the protein (chicken), and save the spud for last. Why? This way you are not eating more carbohydrates at one time than you should, you will be full quicker by eating both the broccoli and chicken first. I think many of us have been programmed to eat our potatoes or grains prior to eating other food groups. We become full too quickly after eating starches and may not have the room for protein and as usual, the poor vegetables lay on the plate alone. We must change our old eating habits and make sure we get the essential nutrients first and then we can savor the starches last (if you have room for them). It is like going to a fast-food joint and you are munching French fries first and then second guessing on eating the burger with lettuce, tomatoes, and pickles. If you are hungry enough, you will eat the entire meal, but it is best to consume nutrients from foods pertaining more nutrients (yes, even a burger with veggies on the patty do have nutrients). Another example is that you go out to a restaurant and order an entrée with a salad prior to your main course meal. You better eat that salad and not slide the plate off the table like a domestic house cat! Furthermore, once your main course arrives, save those steak fries, rice, or whatever carbohydrates for last to consume. You will become full or nearly full by eating most of your entrée and you can bring home the rest of your food in a doggy bag. Or there is no law for you to complete your entire plate. You can eat what is essential and discard what is not. Sometimes we must play reverse psychology on ourselves to smooth the bumps on the road for a weight loss success. Practicing good habits within a great habit will lead to results *sooner than later.* Overall, it is about staying focused on your goals and the adjustments you make will follow through. Success is not achieved overnight. If we all became overnight success, where would we see the extraordinary in us? Let us all flourish together!

CHAPTER 10

"The food you eat can be either the safest and the most powerful form of medicine or the slowest form of poison."

-Ann Wigmore

A GOOD DIET IS A STAPLE for health and wellness. Having a good diet is detrimental while on your fitness journey. The myth goes that people believe diets are to cut the amount we eat in a day in half to almost zero! That is not necessarily true about all diets. A diet is simply a program to follow while eating food regularly. The diet I chose to lose a significant amount of weight was simple. I focused on eating clean and tracked my calorie intake. Sounds basic enough, right? It should be. You probably heard of gluten-free diets or a keto diet. Other diets to follow are both the Mediterranean and Paleo diets. The South Beach Diet has been popular over the years as well as the Adkin's Diet. Like a pair of jeans, one size does not fit all. Thankfully, there are many diets to choose from. Whatever diet you consider, please do your research. Certain diets may or may not be ideal to be on long-term. I have seen people lose weight from the keto diet, which is a diet consisting of high fat and low carb intake. According to a website called Healthline, the site explains, *"Early evidence [what has been researched] also suggests that this low carb, high fat diet [ketogenic] may help treat certain cancers, Alzheimer's disease, and other conditions. Still, higher quality research is still needed to determine this diet's long-term safety and effectiveness."* If you have a sedentary lifestyle where you do exercise minimally and let us say you work behind a desk, the keto diet may be ideal for you. For instance, having spaghetti for dinner or any cuisine that consists of high carbohydrates is not an idea to consume regularly. If you do exercise and have cut back on carb intake, you can treat a spaghetti meal as a cheat meal. If you are an athlete or a highly active person, you can afford a few more spaghetti dinners each week, especially if you are planning to run a marathon the next day or often partake in high-intensity physical activities. Carbohydrates are sugar molecules which are a source of energy your body needs. On another website called *MedlinePlus*, by the *National Library of Medicine*, the site supplied a great understanding of how carbohydrates are broken down into glucose which supplied the body's main source of energy. One segment from the online site told that, *"There are three main types of carbohydrates which are sugars, starches, and fiber."* I will not go into further detail but please do yourself a favor by learning more about these nutrients and specific diets; it can include a consultation with your physician or reading about these energy sources in health articles and food journals. My goal is to give you, the reader, a general understanding of how carbohydrates affect our bodies. I will share some information that was explained to me by personal trainers over the years. There are various kinds of carbohydrates as the *MedlinePlus* mentioned but there is a breakdown between two types of carbohydrates which are simple and complex. To sustain energy throughout the day, it is recommended to include the intake of complex carbs as part of your daily diet. These complex carbs are whole grains foods such as wheat bread, oatmeal, wheat pasta, and brown rice. Fruits like apples, bananas, and pears are notable examples of complex carbs. Potatoes are an excellent source of energy, especially sweet potatoes. It takes longer for the body to break down the sugar molecules that turn into glucose. Hence forth, that length of time is your energy source. If you do enjoy pasta but do not want to give it up just yet for your weight loss journey, substitute it with brown pasta or pasta made from vegetables and protein (spinach pasta, chickpea pasta). Certain potatoes like russet potatoes are starchy but consuming them in moderation has their benefits. If you enjoy your spuds, substitute white potatoes with sweet potatoes. Just remember that potatoes are naturally healthy until you add butter, sour cream, bacon bits, cheese, etcetera, for toppings! What helped me towards my weight loss success and weight management is to enjoy foods at their bareness or "nakedness." You can add black pepper and parsley to your potatoes. Even a small drizzle of honey and cinnamon are better toppings to have on a sweet potato than brown sugar, butter, and even marshmallows. In the beginning of my journey, these spuds tasted "boring" without all those decadent toppings; nevertheless, I got used to the taste by adapting and creating a habit of healthy eating. Hmm, I also managed to lose fat from doing this as well. It is amazing how many good choices from changing a habit have its benefits! Change? Habit? Have we talked about this before? Simple carbohydrates are the decadent sources of energy that we also consume. Sadly, many people eat simple carbohydrates daily. These simple carbs include *but are not limited to* chocolate bars, energy drinks, white bread, syrups, donuts, pancakes, etcetera... You got the point. These simple carbs will give you that quick "burst" of energy and then the energy quickly goes away which leads you to a hard sugar crash, yikes! If you enjoy your sugary cereals in the morning, replace it with low-sugar oatmeal, it is filling, and you sustain more energy because oatmeal is a complex carb (as previously mentioned). If you love cereal like I do (I could seriously eat cereal for breakfast, lunch, and dinner), I recommend eating a bowl of plain Cheerios or any reduced sugar cereal and add fresh fruit in your bowl for natural sugars. I enjoy my bowl of Cheerios with either blueberries or chopped strawberries. A 1 ½ cups of Cheerios, including skim or low-fat milk, is 140 calories. Be mindful of serving size of whatever food you are eating. You stay within the suggested serving size (or less), chances are you will stay on track towards your fitness goals. Speaking of suggested serving size, let us talk more about calorie tracking. There are multiple applications that you can download on your smartphone (*MyFitnessPal as an example) to keep track of calories you consume throughout the day. Or in "ye olden days" you can have a personal journal and jot down the foods you ate, the servings, and find out what the calories are from the food that was consumed. In the last chapter, I spoke about how there is no law to finish all what is on your plate. It has been programmed in our minds since we were children that we had to finish our plate of food, or we could not go outside and play! You are an adult; you can choose how much you want to consume of what is on your plate. If you do not eat all the food, then you do not consume all the calories. But please, do your parents, your sweet grandma, and me a favor: *at least eat all the vegetables before you go out and play!* I am going to use a banana as an example (again) for serving size and calorie tracking. Depending on the size, bananas can be high in calories and carbs. A medium banana can range around 110 calories, 28 grams of carbs, and 15 grams of *natural* sugars. If you remember, a banana is a complex carb, so this fruit is useful to sustain energy. If you are planning to do the keto diet, you may want to avoid eating a banana as whole and to consume half of it. I have heard through the fitness grapevine that it is recommended to eat only half of a banana (especially a large one) or eat one half in the morning and save the other half for later consumption. You will save yourself on calories and if you decide to finish eating the banana later, you burned enough calories to eat what was left of the fruit. I sometimes follow this theory and sometimes do not. If I run long-distance, I will add a whole banana in my post-protein smoothie. I need to regain energy and use the potassium for its entirety. I suggest that you should follow a diet that best suits your lifestyle needs and keep track of the foods you consume. Have you heard of MACROS? The word MACROS stands for micronutrients. When understanding MACROS, you will have greater success on calorie tracking, losing weight, building muscle, and weight management. An article I read from ActiveBeat, it says that *"[micronutrient] *refers to the process of counting the exact amount of carbohydrates, protein, and fats you consume in any given day.*" This method of tracking is popular amongst fitness enthusiasts and professionals like bodybuilders, CrossFit trainers, marathoners, triathletes, and other athletes. The article also shows a perfect diagram of how the MACROS process works in our food consumption. It is eating a plate of food with a balance of protein, carbs, and good fats (avocadoes, nuts). To figure out how much MACROS, you need to consume enough to lose weight and keep a healthy body weight. A dietitian and a fitness trainer who is also certified as a nutrition coach can teach you how to do this. I will reiterate once more that our bodies differentiate from each other, and these professionals who specialize in nutrition can create a customized plan to fit your dietary and fitness needs. Here is some advice to follow when watching your food intake. You can easily eat a cheeseburger with a small fry for around 600 calories (using easy numbers; calories may fluctuate). Or you can eat a large plate of food consisting of slices of ½ of an avocado, 6oz grilled salmon, 1 cup of cooked spinach, a ¼ cup of grilled pineapple chunks and a light vinaigrette dressing drizzled over the food. You can also wash the food down with a small glass of red wine, yes even wine. This meal could also be around 600 calories but there is a significant difference between the amount of vital nutrients and macronutrients consumed. The other meal of cheeseburger and fry have some nutrients and an unbalanced number of micronutrients. This is based on patty meat (not lean meat either), along with processed yellow cheese, and is placed in between a high calorie, high carb bun. Let us not forget the side of deep-fried, sliced potatoes having elevated levels of sodium and trans fats. I do not know about you, but you get more bang for your buck by eating a plate of decorative, healthy foods than being stuck with one burger and French fries. **When we learn how to appropriate the foods that we eat and how much we eat them, then there is no secret behind which foods to eat in a healthy diet**. We need to educate ourselves about food in general. You can do this by researching through different health periodicals and seeking advice from health professionals. Here is another good tidbit about dieting, it is all in your head. Again, the word diet is not trying to scare you. A diet does not mean you and your spouse must split a pea for dinner. You both might save money on groceries, though! I am kidding, please consume more than just ½ a pea. Nevertheless, weight is lost when reducing calorie intake. Let us say you cut back on your food intake in four weeks (for simple numbers) and lost twenty pounds. Then once you are content with the weight loss, you resume eating generous portioned meals. After a few weeks, you noticed you added a couple pounds or more (your jeans fit more snugged than usual). *What gives?* You thought to yourself. This is the biggest reason people get discouraged when "dieting." Results, especially instant results, come and go like the wind outside. Also, the first few pounds you do lose are normally water weight and not fat. To lose weight and keep the weight off, you would have to stick to a *strict* diet and continue exercising. Is this the only practical way to support a healthy weight and lifestyle? Not entirely. There is another diet that is popular amongst the social media world called flexible eating. Flex eating is where you normally eat healthy foods and treat yourself to a small guilty pleasure that you love to indulge. A guilty pleasure could be a chocolate chip cookie or a small cake slice. Did these two junk foods ruin your entire diet? Not exactly because you stayed focused on eating healthy up to ninety percent of the time (80/20 to 90/10 rule). I learned about flex eating a few years ago after following some fitness enthusiasts and experts on Instagram. I was in awe of this diet plan, and it only works in your favor if you keep a healthy and active lifestyle. You do have to treat yourself every now and then, one chocolate chip cookie will not destroy your entire weight loss plan. If you were to eat a half dozen chocolate chip cookies, then it becomes a different story. My goodness, I could go on and write for hours on end about dieting and which foods to eat and avoid! We humans already know that eating healthy is essential for a better lifestyle. **We know what to eat and what not to eat; we know how much to eat per meal.** Unfortunately, common sense is not always common. It is falling back into a comfort level that can also keep us ignorant of the truth that is outside of our trained thoughts. We must reprogram ourselves and reach a new level of knowledge to hit our goals. Knowledge is power and we can never stop learning if we are yearning to become better beings. I do have one rant before ending this chapter, the belief of having a "cheat day" is a total sham. This is my opinion, you can take it with a grain of salt but if you are serious on shredding massive weight off, then I would read this section carefully. Cheat days defeats the purpose of tracking calories for total weight loss. A cheat day or cheat days can be any day of the week, the most popular choices are the weekends. From Monday through Friday, you worked your tail off from doing vigorous workouts, tracking your MACROS and reducing your calorie intake each weekday. I am going to throw a number out there but your goal each day is to consume 1,500 calories or less. Then the weekend comes, and your mind is thinking, *oh thank God the weekend is here because eating another turkey taco and chewing down a spinach salad will be the death of me! I want to eat whatever I want because I will have my cheat days!* Have you done that before and more than once? During the week you "deprived" your bodies from guilty pleasures and then all Hell breaks loose come the weekend? STOP THAT RIGHT NOW! Come Saturday, you may be ordering pizza with buffalo wings, drinking a few beers, and enjoying a chocolate molten lava cake. Sure, you may have worked out Saturday morning but the last time I checked, these foods and drinks can be over 3,000 calories and greater. Oh wait, Sunday comes along, and you could be going to a friend's or a family member's house for a large, warm fuzzy feeling dinner. How does Italian food sound to you? Italian food is one of the most popular cuisines to eat, period. Grandma made pasta alfredo and homemade meatballs. That food is not going to eat themselves; someone needs to polish the plate! *Crud, there goes another 1,000 plus calories in dinner alone.* Grandma, I am not knocking your decadent meatballs nor giving Italian food a bad rap (I am partially Italian myself), but we must agree that these aren't the healthiest foods to eat at a large quantity. Over the "fun" weekend, *because these days were your cheat days, and cheat days are fun, while eating healthy is not;* you could have consumed around 10,000 calories! The 10,000 calories would be considered the other meals, snacks, and any drinks you had throughout each day. Do not try this if you do not believe me. I am not encouraging anyone to make mistakes after I give them sound advice, especially since I made these similar mistakes in the past. I believe in a "cheat meal". A cheat meal can be a meal that you choose to indulge on a single serve only. You can have a cheat meal once to twice a week without blowing your diet out of the water. After you eat your cheat meal, you resume eating healthily for the rest of the day. I enjoy my cheat meals as my lunch. I will order some sushi or have a plate of Chicken Kow, *give me chopsticks fast!* Once lunch is over, I resume eating healthily. With a cheat meal, the guilt is not there because you are disciplined enough to return to a healthier diet. I would recommend planning your cheat meals along with your workouts (earn your indulgence). A cheat meal does not necessarily have to be for lunch, it could be your breakfast or dinner. You can pick a day, pick a time, and go treat yourself. Remember, a cheat meal is not terrible if you treat yourself once to twice a week. Cheat meals could look like flex dieting; however, cheat meals are less frequent than having a small cookie or half a donut per day. You are not depriving your body, but you are also rewarding your efforts from living a healthy lifestyle by sparingly eating a decadent meal per week. All. Freaking. Mind. Games. Society has us thinking that there are good and bad foods which intuitively, there's healthy and unhealthy foods to eat; and it does not necessarily mean bad. A slice of cake has some protein, high in sugar and simple carbs, but a slice of salmon has more protein, good fats, and low on carbs. You select your battles. If you want to eat well and become fit, then eat a piece of cake occasionally, but often eat the foods that are favored in your MACROS needs. These decisions of dieting and eating healthily are all in your head. It gets overwhelming which is why I recommend you learn about different diets and choose the diet you want to follow. If you are still stumped, reach out to your healthcare professional or a nutrition coach. They can point you in the right direction. To reiterate in this chapter, losing weight is not all about the hours spent in the gym, but it is understanding how food is processed in our digestive system that helps us overall. I know a few people who have lost weight by watching what they eat and some of them have lost a significant amount of fat. However, there is a new problem: no muscle gain. To feel healthy, you must eat healthily. To feel strong, you must become strong. How you gain strength is decided by how active you are. You will have sustainable energy from eating healthier foods, let us put that energy to beneficial use![3][4][5]

---

[3] *"Carbohydrates" MedlinePlus.gov
MedlinePlus
http://www.medlineplus.gov/carbohydrates.hmtl
Accessed last 18 of Feb. 2022

[4] *"A Guide to Mastering your Macros" ActiveBeat.com
ActiveBeat
http://www.activebeat.com/diet-nutrition/a-7-step-guide-to-mastering-your-macros.com
Accessed last 18 of Feb. 2022

[5] *MyFitnessPal is an application that can be downloaded via smart phone/smart watch/and computer. All copyright material is licensed and registered under MyFitnessPal. For more information about MyFitnessPal, please visit their website at http://www.myfitnesspal.com.

CHAPTER 11

"Fitness establishes a unique bond between our body and spirit, and in the process, we discover strength of one and the depth of the other."

-Unknown

EXERCISING UNTIL YOU ARE FATIGUED can detox your mind, body, and soul. Through my divorce process, going to the gym helped me escape from the daily woes and I would walk out feeling refreshed and thinking clearly. Any negativity and anxiety I suffered through each day would be sweated out of my system. Thanks to the endorphins that were released while working out, I felt a natural "high" throughout the rest of the day. As a school bus driver at the time, I would hit the gym after work since it was on the way home, I had no excuse for not going. Although, I prefer to work out in the morning because it gives me the energy for the day ahead of me. Thankfully, at my current employment in healthcare, I can squeeze in a morning workout prior to my shift. My favorite exercise in the morning is running, especially outside when the air is cooled and calmed. When I first started exercising to the Present Day, the length of time and intensity of my workouts varied throughout the years. When I first started working out, I did lighter activities and took my time (baby steps). As my body transformation progressed, my workout routines became intense, and I wanted to complete specific activities during each session. Until I was used to a pattern of going to the gym or exercising in my free time, I introduced more activities into my new lifestyle. I began long-distance running, Vinyasa yoga, and boxing heavy bag. My current goal for my active lifestyle is to have endurance and strength, especially training for upcoming races. The pursuit of healthy weight management is a constant target for me to aim for. I explained to people that weight management can be more difficult than losing weight. I will use grades as an analogy: you are in school, and your goal is to get a 4.0 GPA. In the first semester, you achieved your goal and received all "As" in your classes. That is wonderful and something worth celebrating. Though, for many students, striving for a 4.0 GPA is particularly challenging and to keep a 4.0 GPA could be a higher level of expectation for all students. Maintaining high grades means even one slip up of scoring a "B" on an exam, can bring down your average. Once again, there is a prominent level of expectation to keep this superb grade point average, like keeping a healthy weight. It is hard to lose weight, but it is extra difficult to keep the weight off. If you have successfully lost weight and want to keep a healthy weight management, just think of weight management as keeping up with your grades. You pretty much know what it takes to get to this point, and it is the matter of keeping your new lifestyle (remember, if this is where you want to be in life, you cannot go back to old habits). I believe that most of my readers bought this book to lose weight and start their own fitness journeys. If you follow the material that is offered in this book, you should be able to get to the point of weight management. This goal is down the road, but it is achievable. My apologies for getting sidetracked but I wanted to include the importance of keeping a new, healthy lifestyle after it has been proven. To prove a healthy lifestyle, we must fall into a pattern of exercising. Once you fall into this pattern, the dread of working out eventually goes away. Why? You created a habit of becoming more active in your life. Eventually, our patterns will hit plateaus, or we will simply become "bored" after doing things repeatedly. I will share with you several activities you can do that will help you reach your goals and give you creativity. Towards the end of 2014 and through 2015, I was working out at least five to six times a week and spent almost two hours at the gym on the weekends. After having this routine for so long, my body was getting "bored" and so was my mind. Luckily, my gym offered studio classes which can help me to become more creative in my workout sessions. I joined several studio classes that were offered at my gym. The first class I joined was Zumba. Zumba is a class that is mixed with cardio and choreography involving different Latin (sometimes pop) genre music. Each Zumba session is normally upbeat, and you move at a fast pace. It is an incredibly fun class and can help you become more coordinated (I was not a graceful dancer prior to Zumba). A similar class that my gym had was

Hip-hop. This class can be intense and sometimes free weights are involved during the choreography segments. Another intense class to take is a weightlifting class. This class, to me, was a love/hate relationship. I enjoyed the fact that the instructor teaches members how to properly lift weights with the correct form. I disliked how difficult it was lifting weights in a demanding environment! It was the speed that made it challenging. Although, you knew you burned calories when you walked out drenched in sweat after each session. I will touch briefly about weightlifting form later in this chapter. HIIT or High Intensity Interval Training is one of the greatest ways to exercise when you are on a time budget. The training involves bursts of high intensity workout and then a rapid cool down to follow. HIIT workouts are thirty second – or – one-minute intervals where you exert as hard as possible and then cool down during the next interval time. You repeat depending on how long your intervals are. You can complete a total workout in twenty minutes with thirty-second intervals or do one-minute intervals for fifteen minutes. Examples of HIIT training are jogging in place, cycling on a stationary bike, jumping jacks, rowing on a machine, and the use of an elliptical. If there is any other exercise that you know you can do intervals in, please do it! The outcome from doing HIIT will leave you sweating, if you do HIIT exercises a few times a week and continue to watch your diet, you should be able to lose weight quickly! If you begin feeling shaky while performing HIIT exercises, **stop at once and rest**. If you are interested in HIIT exercises but not sure how your body will react, I would recommend having a friend join you or asking a personal trainer to oversee your activity. If you have health concerns, you should ask your physician first before performing this activity or any other activities. It does not hurt to be cautious, but it does hurt if you are not! Hiring a personal trainer is another beneficial way to help break up the monotony in your workout routines. You consult with a trainer to create a game plan for losing weight and a trainer will keep you accountable until your goals are met. A trainer's goal is to make sure you hit your goals. They also supervise you over your form when performing activities. They will correct you and show you the proper way of using any gym equipment such as free weights, circuit machines, and cardio equipment. I was offered a free session with a trainer at the gym. This is quite a funny story because I did not use a personal trainer while losing weight. I did take the opportunity and a great trainer at my gym gave me a quick rundown on how to safely use the circuit machines. She did not have to tell me how to achieve my goals because she has seen me workout diligently on a regular basis. I do have one regret while losing all my weight is that I should have bought several training sessions with a trainer. I would have paced myself better by striving to hit my goals and would have avoided injuries from improper workouts. If you do decide to collaborate with a trainer, make sure you take their training seriously, that way you can use what you learned and exercise properly and efficiently while you are on your own. Hitting your goals is not always achieved on someone else's availability; these are your personal goals to conduct. Friends of mine have complimented me on occasions on how much of an inspiration I am to them, especially since they have seen my body transformation. I have had a few friends that joined with me to go workout. They enjoyed picking my brain to find out the quickest way is to lose belly fat and gain muscle. However, doing just one specific workout will not help you achieve your goal of becoming fit altogether. You may have heard of someone mentioned that they did "Leg Day" on Monday and will do "Chest Day" on Tuesday. In a homespun, if you are planning to do weight training every day, it is a smart move to focus one muscle group per session. This will allow most of your body to recover each day. If you would rather do a full body workout, then it is recommended to spend at least two or three days a week training and recover for the rest of the week. If you do not allow your body to recover, then injuries will occur. Once again, I am trying to steer you in the right direction based on the mistakes I have made in the past. That is another error on my end during my fitness journey; I did not listen to my tired body. My tired body wanted to stop listening to me! After losing over 125lbs, I felt chronic muscle soreness. I had to create the habit of using rest days. Confession: I resented rest days! Although, the most fascinating part of rest days is your body is using energy to recover. While using energy, the body is also burning calories. How cool is that? You are still burning calories or having a "workout" while your body is recovering. The physiology of the human body is impressive. You can learn more about muscle recovery and how the human body repairs itself by reading fitness journals. Let us talk about some fitness myths that I have fallen into believing. Doing straight cardio will get you to lose fat and increase stamina. Doing straight weightlifting (strengthening, conditioning) will make you become strong and gain muscle. These are both true, but the myth is that people believe they lose weight by doing cardio only and believe that weightlifting will make a person "buff and bulky". To become a body builder, you do not entirely focus on weightlifting alone, "bulking" happens from following an extremely strict diet plan. Remember about tracking calories and knowing MACROS? A body builder is solely devoted to following a dedicated diet and workout plan to seek the best physical performance. You may be thinking to yourself, *well I am better off doing weight training and avoiding cardio altogether.* To completely throw cardio out the window is absurd thinking! Cardio fitness is a fantastic way to improve endurance and burn fat. On the contrary, include both cardio and weight training in your routine. Did you know that weight training increases your metabolism? Therefore, if you focus on doing both cardio and weight training you will enjoy the benefits from burning fat and having a higher metabolism. Thus, the weight you lose, you can keep the weight off. While going through my journey, one of my fitness friends recommended me to do at least fifteen minutes of weightlifting while exercising (gym or at home). It might not sound much, but in those fitness minutes of strengthening can add up, especially when you are often doing this workout. Also, fifteen minutes will become a longer duration once you figure out what you need to do and what body group you work on. At this point, your body will tell you *that is enough,* or *keep pushing!* I have had people ask me if they should do cardio first then weights or vice versa. Quite frankly, I suggest lifting weights first and finishing your workout with cardio. You do cardio first; you may become too fatigued to do strengthening. However, you can do a brief warmup (five to ten minutes) of cardio to engage your muscles and then start your strengthening sessions. Some people may like to do cardio first and then hit the circuit to do weight training or use free weights. Either way, you are still working out and reaping the benefits from both cardio and weights. Many people split their training schedules with conditioning one day and cardio for the following day. Whatever your plan is, please continue to stick with these routines so you can achieve your fitness goals. I am at the point now where I do more cardio because I love running, *did you know that I enjoy running?* However, I do not run only to enhance my endurance, I also still do some conditioning to help enhance performance by training the entire body. A runner's tip: you do not solely depend on your legs and knees to do all the work while you are out on foot. Your core must be engaged and having strong arms will help propel you on route. Having strong glutes and hip flexors will increase flexibility and decrease the chances of injury. I had to learn the hard way after injuring my hip flexors/groin area on several occasions. The recovery is long term too, at least six weeks or longer. Since my mistakes, I continue to focus on strengthening both my glutes and hips. You can see that weight conditioning is equally as important to cardiovascular endurance. You keep these exercises as part of your pattern, you will lose weight, gain muscle, and feel happier (thanks to endorphins and dopamine)! You may be thinking to yourself, *doing all these different workout routines sound like a chore, I would not know where to begin!* Oh, I agree to an extent on this. Nowadays, we have an array of exercise programs available for us. It can become overwhelming for a beginner who simply wants to become fit and have an active lifestyle. Fortunately, there are videos posted on social media of ideas and creative ways to become physically active. If you have a friend who lives an active lifestyle, ask your friend to exercise together. Studio classes are great at engaging a group of people in a creative and challenging environment. Personal trainers are available to help create a plan for you to reach your goals and keep you on track. This segment of workout ideas is an infinite subject that makes the physiology of the human body so mysterious. With a strong mind you can raise the bar and push your body to the limit; and yes, there is a limit. If it is your first week at the gym or twentieth week, please do not copy the big guy who is deadlifting 500lbs or the petite gal running fifteen miles at a speed of 8 miles per hour on the treadmill, no break. These people are examples of those who have spent years of hard work and dedication to become who they are today. Also, these people who are outperforming the "average Joes" do have a greater chance for injuries. You can push yourself to a certain limit before seriously hurting yourself. **This is one of the biggest reasons that people become discouraged from exercising and will stop working out with the excuse that it is not for them.** If you start out on the lighter side of a fitness regimen, this will allow your body to adjust from being sedentary to becoming regularly active. Like I said earlier, it takes baby steps in the beginning before you can dedicate more time and energy to achieve greater things! In the recent pandemic, people's lives have changed dramatically. We have seen and experienced these changes both in our work life, home life, and social life. Like many businesses during the pandemic, the gyms suffered terrifically without members coming into their facilities. During 2020, my work hours were temporarily reduced, and I took the advantage of running outside and enjoying nature's beauty. During the week, I was able to do seven to eight miles of outdoor running. In my den, I do have an elliptical and some free weights. It was quite nice to be able to work out when I want, my personal gym is open 24/7. You also may have a personal gym and have taken advantage of it while in quarantined. Sometime ago, The Washington Post released an article titled, *"The pandemic's home-workout revolution may be here to stay."* It explained a dramatic shift in the large realm of fitness. Studio classes are streamline and people can do Zoom meetings with their personal trainers and still follow a workout plan at home. The article also told that, *"Yellowstone National Park recorded its busiest September and October on record-and* [Americans] *embraced other outdoor activities to escape the monotony of stay-at-home life."* People have spent thousands of dollars on home gyms including cardio and weight training machines. Peloton has exploded growth in sales in the last couple of years. The Washington Post's article also included, *"The company* [Peloton] *reported revenue of $758 million, a 232 percent increase from the same period of the previous year."* [2019] What has also gained in popularity are internet fitness companies. The same article said, *"... After the Mirror, the maker of the reflective-glass fitness device, was acquired by Lululemon Athletica, it expected to have ended 2020 with $150 million in revenue, up from the previously projected $100 million in revenue, according to company forecasts."* These are just a few companies that have done extremely well during the turbulent pandemic times. We can safely say that there is no excuse for not exercising and staying active in whatever times our world is in. The technology most people have is at their fingertips by downloading fitness apps and accessing many online fitness sources. Eventually, the gyms and fitness clubs were able to be reopened and have followed a sanitary protocol to keep both members and staff relatively safe from covid and other airborne viruses. Outdoor activities are great opportunities to enjoy the scenery and burn calories while on the move. We can reap the rewards from all these opportunities if we decide to do so. You could say the pandemic has given people greater opportunity to achieve their fitness goals and dreams![6]

---

[6] *"The pandemic's home-workout revolution may be here to stay" The Washington Post
The Washington Post
http://www.washingtonpost.com/road-to-recover/2021/01/07/home-fitness-boom/
Accessed last 21 of Feb. 2022

CHAPTER 12

"It has to be hard, so you'll never forget."

-Bob Harper

EMBARKING ON A JOURNEY has changed my life for the greater good. The journey has enabled me to overcome the hardships in my life while transforming into a person that I have wanted to become for a long time. I now embraced those hardships because it shed a light of hope to design a new future. Also, I pursued happiness that I can find only in myself. You would think changing your life for the better will take decades to complete, but if you are driven enough, creating a new life can be completed in a shorter time. In April of 2014, that was the tipping point to alter my life if I wanted to be happy. It was also the last time I saw myself weighing almost 300lbs. This frightened me enough to change my ways. Upon my obesity and hitting rock bottom, this gave me the ultimatum to do something about it. **Sometimes, life might need to**

scare you enough to make things right. I would like to share another story that relates to fear and hope. Fifteen years ago, I worked for a large financial firm. I was an independent contractor and mostly worked on commissions and residuals. Despite leaving the financial group years later, I gained knowledge of money management and business operations. Several times each year as a contractor, we went to business seminars and conventions. I remember taking part in a workshop that talked about personal motivation-*what are people's "why" that motivates them to become successful?* The instructor explained the diverse ways people are motivated to achieve their goals. Some people may achieve goals better if they know there are incentives. Other people achieve goals out of fear of failure or wanting to change their situations. Then, there is a group of people who fall into both categories. It was one of the most striking things I learned from that workshop. Looking back, I realized I was more motivated to hit my goals by fear. I was already afraid that my life was upside down and if I did not help myself, it would only get worse. I was not so motivated to lose weight to fit in a string bikini or to look like a supermodel. If I really wanted to fit comfortably in a string bikini, I would have lost weight years ago prior to things hitting the fan. It was not my *"why"*. My *"why"* was the fear of the mishaps I faced which drove me to change my life for the better. From being in despair, I had nothing else to lose besides weight! Let us brainstorm ideas of what motivates you to hit your fitness goals. **What is your "why"?** Do you want to feel better about yourself every time you look into a mirror? Or do you want to lose enough weight and gain muscle so you can move around better? Is *"your why"* to improve your overall health and wellbeing?

Or do you simply want to wear a new wardrobe consisting of smaller attire? Are you currently going through obstacles in your personal life and want to change for the better? We know there are multiple reasons why people want to lose weight and they know what motivates them to do so. I learned through my personal hardships and pain, that I had to improve my mental health and everything else would follow through. Your *"why"* needs to be so significant in your life that you will do whatever it takes to achieve it. **Is your *"why"* big enough to motivate a lifestyle change?** How bad do you want to lose weight? How serious are you about starting a weight loss journey? Do you believe you can stick to it once you have started? In March of 2015, I became *happily divorced* and lost eighty pounds in almost a year. In May of 2015, I finally lost one-hundred pounds of weight! When I shared the news at the gym of my hundred-pound weight loss, the manager there helped me celebrate by having me carry two 50lb dumbbells and walk several steps. Odd way to celebrate, right? He wanted to illustrate that my body carried a hundred pounds of excess weight- is that not crazy? It shows the burden that our bodies endure when we carry around more weight than we should. I was happy to reach this milestone, but I told myself that I had twenty-five pounds more to lose. I was inches away from the finish line! In the fall of 2015, I finally reached the finish line and lost 125lbs. Based on experience, the first twenty-five pounds and the last twenty-five pounds are the toughest to lose. My theory on this is getting the ball rolling and keeping what is left of the ball rolling to the finish line! The fall of 2015 was very memorable and rewarding. In September, I completed my first 5k race and finished it under 29 minutes, I averaged over nine minutes a mile! In October, I networked with a local supplement shop and the owner presented a story of my body transformation on social media. I felt amazing during this time, I reaped the rewards from the demanding work that I have done. Just think, it took almost two years to complete a body transformation. I weighed 264lbs in April of 2014 to 139lbs in October of 2015. *Incredible.* This can be you too! To complete a body transformation, it does not take as long as you think if you are willing to be dedicated and work hard. If it takes you longer than two years, that is okay! Until you say that you have lost enough weight or have achieved your fitness level, then you have crossed the finish line. The numbers will speak for themselves. Speaking of numbers, let us go over some: do you recall in the beginning of the book, that the first time I lost weight, I weighed 143lbs and wore size 9 in jeans? Nowadays, I wear size 4 jeans and weigh about the same. You might be asking yourself, *how is that possible? If you weigh a certain amount, you are destined to wear a certain size.* This is not necessarily true. Height and weight do play a factor that can decide the size of your apparel, but **body sculpting** or "toning" plays a role in the actual size that we are. Body sculpting takes place while doing mostly weight conditioning and dieting. When I was a size 9 and weighed 143lbs, I did not have much muscle; and still had plenty of fat. At fourteen years of age, I was not focused on weightlifting but went mostly on walks, rode my bicycle around the neighborhood, rode horses, and followed a strict diet. Hence, I lost a tad of weight, but my body still seemed "flabby." I did not "tone" or sculpted my body. We talked in the last chapter of the benefits of weightlifting because it redefines your shape. Muscle weighs more than fat mass, hence your body has a lovely way to sculpt your physical shape. Over the years, I have been focused on weight management (keeping my GPA up), and people have accused me of weighing less than I am! We know looks are deceiving and the bathroom scale does a satisfactory job of how much you appear to weigh. The scale can only do so much justice. The scale does not factor in water retention, food you have consumed the day before, sleep, clothing, relieving yourself, muscle mass, etcetera. I know when I go do my long-distance running, the water that I have drank during my run, is sweated out. For kicks and giggles, I will go on my bathroom scale after running, and noticed I am about three pounds less than I originally weighed on the same day. As soon as I recover and eat meals, the three pounds comes back. It just shows that the scale isn't always correct on how much you physically weigh. There is another measurement to figure out the size of our bodies and that is called Body Mass Index or BMI. The National Heart, Lung, and Blood Institute describes BMI, *"... *a measure of body fat based on height and weight that applies to adult men and women."* The online source has a chart to measure your height and weight. When I weighed 264lbs, my BMI was over 46%, which is considered *morbidly obese.* Just the thought of knowing to be morbidly obese was depressing; really, there are not enough words to describe the feeling! I have kept my BMI at around 23% since my body transformation. Depending on the height of a person, this is considered average weight. To figure out your BMI, there are BMI calculators available to figure out your body size. You can also visit your doctor's office to receive a measurement and the clinical staff can give you a total run down how BMI measures our bodies. Personal trainers also have this measuring tool available, especially for your consultation and last session to see progress. There is a flaw with BMI measuring body composition which does not specifically factor in muscle mass and excess skin. Excess skin is loose skin from aging and weight loss. For the most correct measurement of your body composition, having skin removal will give you better numbers. Loose skin or excess skin will appear once you lose a significant amount of weight. I know this from experience. After you lose weight, some of your skin may form back to its original shape but excess skin may not have the elasticity and will continue to hang over your body. You can improve some of the elasticity by doing body sculpting. The most effective way to remove loose skin is to do skin removal surgery. In January of 2022, I had a panniculectomy and abdominoplasty (tummy tuck) which removed about three pounds of excess skin off my abdomen and pelvis. The post recovery was intense, yet I am incredibly happy with my results. Having these surgeries performed is not for the faintly hearted and you should consult with your doctor if these surgeries are right for you, especially after weight loss. Surgeries of any sort have their risks and it is a clever idea to do research before going under the knife. However, to have excess skin versus to still be morbidly obese, I would rather have some loose skin! Skin removal surgery is not for everyone. For some people, maybe you, who need to drop just a few pounds, you can have your skin get its elasticity back by doing weightlifting, which is fortunate to hear. There are those, like me, who had lost so much weight, the skin removal surgery may be a thought to have in mind. Before reaching this stage of weight loss, we need to make sure we hit our goals first.

After having skin removal surgery or no surgery, do not think that it is the end of staying active. You need to stay active to keep your new lifestyle. Your new lifestyle will end if you choose to do so. Keep in mind, what you fought for to avoid what was in your past, could come back. Do not forget that we have two paths to choose from. One path trailed in the dark and the other path was hazy, but the sunshine made everything visible at the end. Each path is available to you so trek *wisely*. Your *"why"*, if big enough, will keep you disciplined for a long time. Success and failures do come and go; but be diligent to continue succeeding. You cross the finish line one time, but you continue winning by moving forward and never looking back.[7]

---

7 *"Calculate Your Body Mass Index" National Heart, Lung, and Blood Institute
U.S. Department of Health and Human Services
https://www.nhlbi.nih.gov/health/educational/lose_wt/BMI/bmicalc.htm
Accessed last 22 of Feb. 2022

CHAPTER 13

WISDOM IS AS VALUABLE as lessons to be learned. That is something to look forward to when getting older. We can pass down our knowledge that we have learned from earlier mistakes and successes to the next generation of curious minds. It is a courteous gift that our senior community has supported us while figuring out how life works. However, not all wisdom is passed down from our parents, grandparents, or great-grandparents. We sometimes cross paths with people who share their wisdom from the tribulations that they have met in the past. Wisdom is worn as a badge of competency, it signifies that "I have been there and done that, and this is what I learned." It is always great to get a piece of advice from those who were in your shoes. People are quite thoughtful by sharing with each other an insight to spare head-aches and setbacks in whatever situation someone might be in. After the dusts settles, we are all born in the same world that is full of curiosity and adventures. We make life just a bit simpler while spreading wealth of wisdom. In one of the final chapters in this book, I want to share more insight with you when it comes to a lifestyle change. It was something I had to figure out on my own and hopefully will help you if you must cross these bridges like I have. Not all these things are bad but think of it as *Cliff's Notes*. Can you recall a time as a young pupil, you had to read a research paper or multiple chapters in a textbook to find the answers to questions that were given to you from the teacher? As a student, you felt that you wanted to read the summary about the topic to save time than reading the entire subject in the textbook. Though, summaries do an excellent job of supplying a general explanation of the material; yet reading the entire article gives you detailed in-formation that supplies the *"why"* as a general explanation. I could have drafted a five-page essay explaining how to simply lose weight. You know, something that gets to the point, and not wasting any-more of your time reading. Although, the key part in this para-graph is *"simply."* This entire book explains a larger picture than weight loss or getting in shape. It explains more than the number of minutes exercising or counting every gram of food on your plate. If you do not consider everything else that plays a role in a success-ful weight loss, it will become difficult for you to reach your goals and keep a better lifestyle. I did not have to share my personal story, talk about making changes, experiencing plateaus, having an inner circle, or any other stuff. I could have just shared quick tips or *tricks* and be done. The material that I drafted into this entire book is *effective* to weight loss and a lifestyle change. **Effectiveness drives results.** You have a desire to lose weight and become fit. You yearn to have a new lifestyle. If you want to change your body and your life, there is a greater explanation that is beyond summarizing the fundamentals. I hope by now, you have a better grasp in the realm of losing weight and changing your life. If you do not understand the key roles to a successful healthy lifestyle, you will return to old habits. Here is some insight I want to explain to you about changing eating habits. I was a fan of milk, and I thought I would "save the calories" by drinking one percent or skim milk. You cannot sugarcoat the fact that milk is not entirely healthy, dairy holds certain constituents that are not practical to consume in our daily diets. Dairy milk has growth hormones, additives, and pardon to be gross but has some bodily substances which came from the animal. There are dairy brands that do produce better quality dairy where their labels mention no additives or growth hormones. I support the initiative to make better choices when making these products and with it, it costs more to produce which leads to higher prices when shopping for them at the supermarkets. The average cost for milk is quite costly and buying a better quality of milk will be several dollars extra. Once I began losing weight, I switched from dairy milk to soymilk and nut-milk. The taste was something I had to grow accustomed to but switching to these nondairy drinks has helped me shed fat, and still received quality amounts of calcium. For one, these nondairy alternatives have less calories than drinking regular milk. A cup of unsweetened almond milk is roughly thirty calories compared to over one hundred calories of two percent low-fat milk. I usually drink unsweetened vanilla almond milk. This milk mixes well in my protein smoothies, baking, and in cereal. Also, nut-milk is gut sensitive. I feel the difference between drinking non-dairy and dairy milk, even if the dairy milk is lactose free. Some non-diary alternatives do have additives and there are varied brands to choose from without these additives. Also, if you have food allergies, especially to nuts, you should ask your physician or an allergist to see if there are other alternatives to consuming non-dairy products. You can also take supplements to get your nutrients which are mostly found in both dairy and non-dairy products. I will make some exceptions on several dairy products: Greek or Scandinavian yogurt is healthy to consume often. Greek yogurt for an example has probiotics which helps the improvement of a healthy digestive tract. Greek yogurt is high in protein and can be low-fat depending what kind of yogurt you look to eat. Scandinavian or *Skyr (pronounced Skeer)* works like Greek yogurt and supplies the same benefits. From what I have experienced, the difference between the two yogurts is that Skyr has a very thick texture (thicker than Greek yogurt). It all depends on the milkfat for these products, if you have a problem with texture, you could try a nonfat Greek or nonfat Skyr yogurt. Lower fat yogurts are runnier than the whole fat yogurts. Cottage cheese is also healthy to consume if you do not mind the texture either. Cottage cheese varies from nonfat to whole fat. Hard cheeses like parmesan are healthy to eat in moderation. If you have a sensitive gut like me, you may need to avoid certain foods, including healthy foods to avoid negative reactions. I have a chronic condition called gastroparesis. If I try eating foods that are high in fiber and high in fat, I will experience abdominal pain and nausea. Gastroparesis is a gastroen-terology disorder where it slows down your digestive tract. When I was diagnosed in 2018 (there are specific tests to confirm diagnosis) I had to follow a low fat, low fiber diet to avoid any flareups. I continued to this day to follow this diet, or I would be feeling sick all the time. Another diet I had to do but was temporary is the low FODMAP diet. This diet helps reduce abdominal pain, nausea, gas, and other gut sensitivities. FODMAP is described from Wikipedia as, *"fermentable oligosaccharides, disaccharides, mono-saccharides, and polyols which are a short chain carbohydrate that are poorly absorbed in the small intestine and are prone to absorb water and ferment in the colon."* Another website, www.dietvs-diease.org published an article that also explains the FODMAP diet, and the site supplies a detailed chart of foods that are considered safe to eat or not safe to eat if you suffer from any gut intolerances or disorders. Sometimes it does not hurt to follow a low FODMAP diet to find out which foods you have problems tolerating. You might be eating healthily for a while and losing weight. However, if you are in chronic discomfort, then try the low FODMAP diet to see which food culprits could be giving you grief. You can also seek a gastroenterologist to find out more about gut sensitivities. The specialist will help you seek solutions to these issues. A happy gut is a healthy gut! Another frequent consumption that many of us (especially Americans) are guilty of eating is fast food and fried food. I am not searching for sources to show stats of the amount of fast food consumed per year; the news networks and social media both do an excellent job making us feel guilty from eating fast food almost daily. Luckily, major fast-food chains have realized that people want healthy options on their menus, and have introduced an array of healthier meals to choose from. It has been years since I ordered from a greasy joint, I know if I were to try to eat a burger, I would feel sick. When you stop eating these foods, you will suffer some abdominal discomfort because your stomach is not used to the high fat content. It is best to avoid these food products as much as possible or eat it very sparingly. Though it is great that there are healthier items on the menu to choose from, if I were to eat something on the go, I would order a PLAIN baked potato from Wendy's and a side salad. If grilled chicken is a possibility, I would order that along with my meal and eat it without the bun or half the bun. Yet, with the baked potato, you are better off without the toppings and for the side salad, pick a nonfat or low-fat dressing. The dressing packet for the salad is the recommended service size to use. A myth with salads is that they are "always" healthy. This is not always true because toppings or heavier dressings will increase the number of calories and fats. Some of these "loaded" salads can have as many calories as a double beef burger! When you order salads, especially at a restaurant, ask the server what is specifically in the salad (if not listed on the menu) and see if you can substitute the toppings with healthier options or have some toppings removed. Deep fried foods are bad. Period. Need I say more? You know it is bad; if you removed the crunchy skin off a fried chicken breast, it does not mean you are safe. The food was still dropped in a deep fryer, those trans fats and oils go beyond the golden crust skin. If you beg to differ and cannot lose your grasp on this crunchy, greasy pleasure, then eat the food sparingly. In all honesty, it is not a good move at all. During my "Fat

Girl Phat Days" (I humorously like to call this stage of my life when I ate whatever I wanted and was obese in doing so), I was able to clean off an entire box of breakfast sausage links. They were so delicious; I could tell I was eating it often because my body circumference was expanding. Fried and greasy foods not only affect your weight, but they also have other health risks. I am giving you tough love here; you will not miss fried foods once you have created a habit of healthy eating. While losing weight, I did substitute my love for bacon with turkey bacon. Obviously, there is a difference between both tastes and calories, but it satisfied me in the interim. Eventually, I quit eating turkey bacon and other processed meats. Processed meats like deli meats are typically lean but have additives. You can get deli meats without nitrates or reduced sodium but when you research how deli meat is processed, you might turn the other cheek like I have. This is my opinion, but consuming lean deli meats can help you with weight loss, just be mindful of how they are made. Did you know that when you are going through a body transformation, your taste buds change too? Yes! You may have added salt to your already salty soup or added marshmallows and brown sugar to your sweet potato, but when you eat food at its bareness, you can naturally taste the sweet and savory of these foods. You will learn to enjoy eating more vegetables, leaner meats, or whatever foods that you normally haven't consumed prior to your healthy lifestyle. Many foods hold sodium, especially soups and hot entrees at restaurants. Do yourself a favor and you can reduce the sodium in a soup by adding water (diluting). You can also tell the server to have your meal have little to no sodium (if possible). Minor changes like this can help reduce your blood pressure and your doctor may give you a high five at your next office visit. Do you have a sweet tooth? I have a sweet tooth. I enjoy sweet things over savory things. Do you know what is not sweet? Having a belly ache from eating sugary candies and pastries. Oh, and these foods are also simple carbohydrates. You will get that instant sugar rush and crash faster than a fallen vase. I could be exaggerating but the feeling of a sugar crash is horrible. You are better off eating natural sugars that are found in fruits. Your taste buds will get accustomed to the natural sweet taste of a pear than eating a large lollipop. Also, fruits are complex carbs, and your energy will sustain longer (your vase will stay on the table, longer). It is an innovative idea to watch your sugar intake, it can prevent you from having health problems in the future. With all this wisdom to consider, always believe that your body is the temple to your soul. Treat your body well. A healthy body with a healthy mind leads to a happy soul. *Oh boy, oh boy, oh boy...what else can I talk about that needs to be removed from your diet to promote healthy eating and weight loss?* There is too much. I have cut soda out of my diet and that has helped me lose weight. Diet soda is not anything better besides having no sugar and zero calories. Let us not forget how soda is made and that you are better off chugging down water than a cherry cola. Alcohol consumption is empty calories meaning you are not receiving many benefits from it unless you want to forget last night. I am not telling you to stop drinking, if you enjoy a glass of wine each night or having a beer over a weekend, then go for it. Dark wines have some health benefits, but in moderation... If it is urgent for you to lose pounds, I would cease drinking for a while until you meet your goal. You can consume drinking again, *in moderation.*

Do you know what beverage that has zero calories and aids in weight loss? Water, and drink plenty of it! Drink enough water to keep your body hydrated and moving. The Mayo-Clinic has a great article called *"Water: How much should you drink every day?"* The online source thoroughly explains that there is a certain amount of water intake for men and women. These daily fluid intakes differentiate between the two sexes. The Mayo-Clinic said, *"The U.S. National Academies of Sciences, Engineering, and Medicine determined that an adequate daily fluid intake is: About 15.5 cups (3.7 liters) of fluids a day for men and about 11.5 cups (2.7 liters) of fluids a day for women."* The website continued suggesting that drinking eight glasses of water per day may be too much or not enough for some people, depending on vigorous activities like exercising, living in a hot environment (desert or subtropical to tropical), proper amount for toxin elimination, and for those who are pregnant or breast feeding. These are exampling that quantity of water must be consumed more often to be both healthy and hydrated. I start off each morning drinking at least a cup of water. I drink as much water as I can before meals; it helps prevent overeating. When I go to a restaurant, the server normally leaves a pitcher of water at the table for my access (too many steps back and forth to refill my glass). Water keeps a clear mind and helps the elasticity of the skin. We know there are many benefits of drinking water. Yet, over drinking can become harmful for us too. If you enjoy quenching your thirst with water, drink as much as you physically can and spread the intake throughout the day, therefore your body can properly drop the excess amount. Make sure you are adamant about your water intake while you are striving to hit your weight loss goals and becoming more fit. One last thought on healthy eating and I promise *(fingers crossed)* this is my final piece of the *pie- in moderation*. The realm of daily consumption. Have you lost weight by not eating? *Of course, who has not lost weight by not eating?* Usually, the decision to lose weight without eating is normally a red flag for eating disorders. These problems are serious, and I am not advising any of my readers to follow suit. Yet, there is a safe practice of not consuming food in a period which is called intermittent fasting. For most adults, fasting is very daunting and often dreadful, especially for someone who needed to fast for certain bloodwork and preoperative procedures. Although, fasting does not necessarily have to be a punishment for your body. Throughout recent studies, health experts have found that intermittent fasting has many benefits for both body and mind. In an article called, "Intermittent Fasting: What is it, and how does it work?" by John Hopkins Medicine, fasting is described as, **"an eating plan that switches between fasting and eating on a regular schedule. Research shows that intermittent fasting is a way to manage your weight and prevent-or even reverse-some forms of disease."* This source has an amazing and detailed explanation of how crucial it is in timing your daily food intake. In my book, it has been mentioned several times what to eat and how much to eat will dictate having good or poor health; yet *when to eat* is part of healthy living. In modern times, many people stay up longer to watch television, browse through the internet, skim through social media, and enjoy other forms of entertainment. Hence, people will tend to snack more and consume food at all hours of the night. Have you snacked right before laying down to sleep or eat in bed? I bet the next morning you felt bad and sluggish. The rule of thumb is to finish your last meal two hours before going to bed. This allows your digestive track to breakdown the foods easier and efficiently distributes nutrients throughout your body. There are several ways to fast. There is a 16:8 approach where you eat in an eight-hour window and fast for sixteen hours (sleeping is included in this long stretch of hours). Another fasting method is the 5:2 approach where you pick two days out of the week to consume only 500-600 calories per day. For myself, I practice the 12:12 approach. You eat within twelve hours (or less if you choose) and fast for twelve hours. This approach is more doable especially for someone who is highly active and needs to consume calories to sustain energy and for muscle recovery. An example of this fasting method is to finish your last meal or snack at 7pm and fast the twelve hours and consume food again at 7am the following day. It does not seem as daunting as you think, correct? If you were to stop eating at 9pm, your next meal would be at 9am the following day. For the 16:8 approach, your last meal could be at 8pm tonight and your next meal to eat is 12pm tomorrow. People can fast for twenty-four hours through seventy-two hours. To me, I called this method radical fasting. It could lead your body into "starvation" mode. If you are willing to complete something like this, cease your activity level, that way you are sustaining your energy. Besides losing weight, the benefits of intermittent fasting can improve physical performance and can enhance both cognitive thinking and memory. It also helps with any tissue repair of the body and protects organs from chronic diseases including diabetes and IBS (irritable bowel syndrome). According to the article, intermittent fasting can also protect people from various cancers. This sounds like a practical method to do daily, especially you can mostly fast in a period by simply sleeping. I noticed my workout activities have improved while fasting. If I am not running long-distance, I will practice fasting while running shorter distances. If I know I will be adding mileage, I carry a snack for extra energy. It is all timing. According to the same article by John Hopkins, intermittent fasting is also not for everyone. People who struggle with blood pressure, or sugar levels, are recommended to avoid extended periods of fasting. Women that are pregnant and nursing should avoid fasting too. If intermittent fasting sparks your interest, ask your doctor about the plan and see if it is recommended for you. A quick tip before we move on to the next section: when you feel hungry while fasting, drink plain water or black coffee to keep you feeling "full." Let me be specific on this: it is considered fasting when you drink plain water (no flavor added, no fruit added) and plain, black coffee (no creams, milk, or sugar added). Let us all go into more detail about coffee. I like to compare coffee to a potato. Coffee is healthy for you until you add all the extras in, same with a potato. We talked about this in earlier chapters, the same thought process applies to drinking coffee. Drinking black coffee has "perks" besides becoming perky from the caffeine. It speeds up the body's metabolism which aids in weight loss. It helps with cognitive thinking and improves memory. Unfortunately, you lose some of these "perks" once milk, cream, sugar, whipped cream, and other guilty pleasures are added to these drinks. Your cup of black coffee went from 5 calories to 200 calories after the "toppings" are added in the cup. Some of these fancy brews can have over 400 calories, which is compared to having a meal! If you are looking to lose weight but still love your favorite brew, substitute the extras with lighter choices like almond milk or sugar free syrup. The best way to lose weight is drinking coffee plain. A healthy lifestyle is not limited to diet plans, it is also about staying active: Let us go over some examples! In your current state, (prior to weight loss, losing weight, or after weight loss) how often do you move around? When the workday is over and you come home, do you normally sit in your favorite recliner for a couple of hours? Do you do house chores? Or do you grab a pair of roller blades and go out roller blading in the park until dusk? If you answered, "yes" to the last question, I give you credit to have enough energy to do laps at the park after work. It must be all that black coffee you have been drinking while fasting. Whatever answer you do have, the question comes down to: **Are you moving around enough?** Moving around does not mean you are running from point "A" to point "B" or skipping around in your house or at work (people might question about you when skipping everywhere but who are they to judge?). I defined moving around as you are getting your steps in. Besides workouts and physical activities, let us not forget that getting your steps in each day is considered being active. To count your steps, you can wear a tracker. Trackers are available at almost any store and are something you can clip on to your pants while you are moving. Nowadays, we have trackers as a feature in our smart phones, smart watches, and fitness watches (Fitbit, Garmin as examples). I normally wear a Garmin and keep track of the steps I do daily. You earn steps while using the stairs too. To increase your steps, try to use the stairs more at your work or in the malls or anywhere that have stairs available. You can also increase your steps by parking further away from a building before entering too. The average goal to hit is 10,000 steps per day. For some, they can have a goal less than this and for others, they can have a higher goal. Either way, when you focus on getting your steps in for the day, you are staying active and burning more calories. *A body in motion, stays in motion*. I hope this chapter has given you a clearer picture of why it is significant to keep focused and motivated after you make a lifestyle change. Some of the tips shared are simply wisdom that I have learned from successes and mistakes I had. My goal was to share tips on methods of dieting and making better food choices to eat. Staying motivated is crucial in losing weight and after weight loss. You use drive, your motivation, to achieve all your goals. Having an active lifestyle becomes relatively easier once you figure out your *why*. Your dreams become a reality with a plan and fortitude.[8][9][10]

---

[8] *"Low-FODMAP diet" Wikipedia
En.m.wikipedia.org
https://www.en.m.wikipedia.org/wiki/Low-FODMAP_diet
Accessed Last 24 of Feb. 2022

[9] *"Water: How much should you drink every day?" Mayo-Clinic, Nutrition and healthy eating
Mayoclinic.org
https://www.mayoclinic.org/healthy-lifestyle/nutrition-and-healthy-eating/in-depth/water/art-20044256#:~text=The%20U.S.%20National%20Academies%20day%20day%20for20%-women
Accessed Last 24 of Feb. 2022

[10] *"Intermittent Fasting: What is it, and how does it work?" John Hopkins Medicine, Food and Nutrition
Johnhopkinsmedicine.org
https://www.hopkinsmedicine.org/health/wellness-and-prevention/intermittent-fasting-what-is-it-and-how-does-it-work
Accessed Last 12 of Mar. 2022

CHAPTER 14

"Motivation is what gets you started; habit is what keeps you going."

-Unknown

THE LIFE YOU DESIRE ONE DAY is soon for you. To say you cannot find the motivation to achieve weight loss success is allowing excuses to justify your actions. Why prevent the future you want simply because you are afraid of the unknown? Your comfort zone must be compromised and can be done when you step out of the box and begin transforming your life. Do not wait until you are fifty pounds lighter to begin the journey. Do not say, "Oh I will be so happy once I can fit into smaller outfits." Or "I will love myself more once I no longer shop at plus-sized department stores." **Your self-worthiness is as important as the person who is reading this right now.** Your first accomplishment should be loving yourself first, and always. You are a great person. I believe so because you like remarkable things in your life, and you want to excel in whatever you decide to take part in. So many people keep imagining what it would be like to be "skinny" and to feel healthier than they feel currently. To change their current lifestyle is daunting and these wishes can feel like a pipe dream. Believe me, I have been at this point before, for a duration of my life. I wished to become fit and see a healthier version of myself but taking the first step felt like a giant leap. I lacked competency and the confidence to believe my dreams can come true. Sometimes, the universe will confront you with alterations that leave you to find a new outlook in life. Do not wait for happiness at the end of your personal fitness journey. While on my journey, I became elated because I morphed into a person that I wanted to become (physically and mentally). Do not get me wrong, I am satisfied since I have lost a tremendous amount of weight. Going out socializing and clothes shopping is more enjoyable for me, but my elation was greater when I noticed the transformation of my body. It could be because I was doubtful to see any "real" results from the work I was committed to doing. If you have the blinders on and stay focused on your goals, your confidence will change once you see results. Do not forget, others are watching too. Your support is there, they are cheering you on while you approach the finish line! *You don't stop! You won't stop! You can't stop!* Your life depends on it! I may not know you but in ways, I feel that we know each other. We know we have shared the same inspirations, goals, and desires for better health. We know the struggles that life throws us at any given time. *We know we are not alone.* I know that I can lose weight and so can you. You can achieve this great endeavor. There is no secret to losing weight, it is about our lifestyles and the choices we make daily that can either improve our health or abolish it. We need to be disciplined to diet and exercise. There is no secret to all this. I understand that there are gastric surgeries and so-called "magic pills" that aid in weight loss; but the experts who suggest these options still encourage the seekers to adapt to a healthy lifestyle. **You cannot return to old ways and attempt to eat right and exercise.** You can start a good habit, my friend. Habits start, end, and change all the time. It takes a short amount of time to form a new habit. Just a brief time, not a *millennium*. Yes, I am exaggerating, but the challenging work may feel like it takes forever to do *(If you believe it will)*. Do not be afraid to get your feet wet. How do you get into a swimming pool? Do you nosedive in or make a huge splash from a cannon ball? Or do you grab the handlebars along the edge of the pool and take steady steps when you walk down the pool ladder? It does not matter because you made it in the pool. The cool water feels refreshing against your skin on a hot, summer's day. Regardless of how you got into the water, you are satisfied to be in. No matter how fast or slow you reach your fitness goals, you are satisfied because you made the journey. **This journey is made for you.**

CHAPTER 15

"It always seems impossible until it's done."

-Nelson Mandela

THE OBSTACLE AHEAD OF YOU is there to assess your ultimate strength. There will never be a perfect time nor a perfect environment to start going after your dreams. Imagine where you will be in one month, three months, six months, and a year from now. Are you willing to change old habits, become accountable for your actions, plan out your journey, and take the first step on the unbeaten path? You can hit your goals and achieve what you want in life with determination. A disciplined mind can break mental barriers. Remove the blindfold that your mind has you wear and evaluate yourself to achieve absolute greatness. The truth of losing weight is that it affects the person beyond physical appearance. There is a spirit that has grown in confidence, competence, mental strength, and *love*. How could you not gain these traits while persevering each day to conquer your goals? Weight loss is both unforgettable and remarkable. The journey to weight loss is unforgettable and remarkable. Ordinary people can achieve what is unforgettable and remarkable. Would this make people extraordinary? I would say so! Are you capable of becoming extraordinary? Absolutely! Do you see yourself achieving the extraordinary? With the blinders off, yes you can. There is an old sales saying, *"If you tell the customer to believe in the product, they will not buy. But if the customer tells you they believe in the product, they will buy."* You as the reader can lose weight, but you may not believe me. You tell yourself you can lose weight, and you will believe that you can. Everything comes down to believing in yourself. Have affirmations for yourself, put your positivity into action and start. What is going on in between your ears will decide what your body follows. Prior to my weight loss success, I had pity for myself. I played victim from my insecurities and believed that I would not become a better person. If I were to keep these negative thoughts flowing around in my mind, it would not have led me to where I am today. The best lessons I learned came from obstacles and mishaps that I had. I learned to *never settle for less!* Life can supply opportunities when the storms are around. Opportunities are always knocking but it is up to us to open the door and let them in. My mishaps could have kept me in the shadows. Instead, I chose to break through and rebuild a brighter future. This was possible when I learned to love myself first. Yes, love makes the world go round. However, to love yourself, your world will go wherever you want it to go. Therefore, please have reassurance of yourself. Those who love you will encourage you to continue your fitness journey. Throughout this book, you learned that plateaus will happen, and setbacks exist. Determination breaks through these barriers. Also, enjoy hitting your goals, either big or small. These achievements do add up in the grand scheme of things. Do you think any minor success is left unseen? *Success is success*, it is noticeable! It is impossible to fool yourself thinking you cannot hit your goals while you have been seeing results along the way. Give yourself some praise; nevertheless, do not throw yourself a pizza party after losing five pounds. Do not indulge too soon because it distracts you from seeing the larger picture. You celebrate your five-pound loss by increasing your motivation. I have seen small victories on a weekly and monthly basis; it motivated me to work harder despite the hurdles I crossed. When I get approached by someone who has heard of my weight loss success, I am asked what my secrets are. I replied, "The secrets are diet, exercise, and being disciplined." The person, stunned, has answered back, "Well, that's not really a secret..." BINGO! There are no secrets to weight loss success! With these three motives, you can put them to the test and see the results. Accountability will keep these motives alive. Changes will help you overcome obstacles and making good habits will keep your fitness journey moving. These skills are tools for you to complete the job. When you have the right tools for the job, the job will get done correctly. These skills aren't something you will find at a hardware store but are assets to the individual. Here is my final analogy of being in the right state of mind, while on your weight loss journey. A nation who continuously has victories on the battlefields will end up winning the war. This also applies to you and me: you (nation) are at war to achieve better health. You will have victories on the battlefield while dieting and exercising.

These victories you earned are weight loss and competence. Losing a battle gives you a setback. When the dust of the gunpowder finally settles, the war is over. When the last drop of sweat and tears dissipate on the floor, your war is over. A peace treaty between nations is a sign of a fresh start. A peace treaty between you and your health is a sign of a new lifestyle. To give up the fight, a white flag is held high enough for the enemy to see. If you give up the fight, the white flag is seen each time you close your eyes-the enemy is you. We are all drafted into a personal war with ourselves. We have a choice to fight or to retreat. Victories are memorable and losses are a given. Only in time, a loss is accepted if you no longer wish to fight. The secret to winning in a war is something that any militants would love to know. The secret to winning your own personal war is to initiate actions for success. In conclusion to this book, you can see that losing weight is not only achievable by diet and exercise. Losing weight is a total mental game. You must mentally prepare yourself to complete your entire journey. Your journey can end at any time once your weight loss goal is met. The next journey is to keep the weight off long-term. Stay dedicated to your new lifestyle. This is a way of life that you are meant to have. I said earlier, if I can do it, then you can do it. If I can change my ways to have the life I wanted, you can do the same. You are worth more than you think. **It is time for you to start going after your goals and dreams.** Are you ready for a lifestyle change? Are you ready to take on the challenges? **Your fitness journey awaits!**

Left: 264lbs 2012 Right: 130lbs November 2019 (first day working in healthcare).

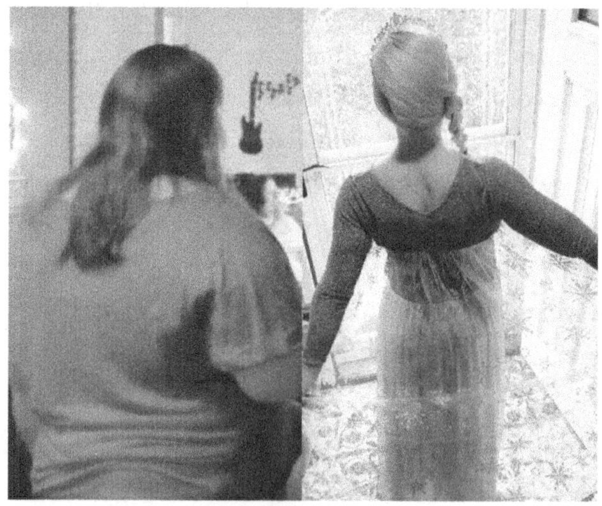

Left: 264lbs 2012 (heaviest) Right picture is of me as Queen Elsa (trademark of Disney) on Halloween in 2018.

Left: 240lbs-250lbs 2009   Right: 143lbs 2022

Left: 210lbs-220lbs 2007   Right: 143lbs 2023

Left: Birthday (8/16/2014) lost 30lbs (234lbs from 264lbs weight loss journey).
Right: 120ish pounds 2018 (I told myself I'll be back in the saddle
once I lost the weight!)

Left: 205lbs (weight loss journey December 2014 59lbs lost)
Right: 143lbs in August 2023, a Chicago Bears preseason game!

Ran my first marathon in December 2022 for St. Jude's Memphis Marathon.
I did it virtual and ran roughly 226 laps around on an indoor track!

Won my first 5k race in November 2022 in my age/gender
category. I finished the race at 28:40secs.

Weight loss journey: Left side: 180lbs or less in 2015.
Right: 143lbs in 2023. I enjoy boxing!

Left: weight loss journey, 2015 (roughly 160lbs). Right: my birthday
(8/16/2020) ran a virtual 10k race during the pandemic. My neighbor showed
me his Gibson Les Paul guitar and a couple years later, I bought it from him!

EPILOGUE

The author of this book tries to depict a series of events involved meeting goals of weight loss success. The goal is for the reader to realize that being in the right state of mind will allow an individual to achieve weight loss and other desires in life. The author has emphasized the importance of making changes and adapting to new, healthier habits. She has explained the psychology behind diets, healthy eating, and exercising. She believes if the reader can learn how food affects our bodies, the reader will make better choices in food consumption. The author also believes that monotony of the same workout routines can slow down progress and create boredom. She reiterates the significance of changing workout routines to avoid plateaus. She also expressed the importance of combining weight training and cardio endurance to achieve fitness goals. She understands there are benefits in both exercise styles. She believes that daily activity can help improve mental wellness and aid in an active lifestyle. To remain adequately active daily, she believes that the reader can hit goals sooner than later. The author drafted this book to share her story of hardships and challenges that she overcame while losing weight. She hopes that her story has explained thoroughly how she conquered the tribulations she endured and stayed persistent for hitting weight loss goals. She wants to inspire people so that they can achieve what they want, especially with being disciplined. She understands that she vaguely explained about food and exercises and used sources to cite stats and definitions of certain material used in some chapters. The author encourages the reader to seek any medical advice from a physician. She also encourages the reader to consult with a personal trainer and health coach to plan out a health and wellness program. She also suggests that the reader can consult with a dietitian about specialty diets. She believes that readers should do research more about health and wellness by reading legitimate sources such as fitness journals and health periodicals. The author of this book shares what she learned from losing weight and shares successes that have helped her. She simply wants to inspire the reader that it is attainable to lose weight by dieting and exercising. She also has told the significance of weight management and keeping a healthy lifestyle to support goals. She realizes she cannot give professional advice but can relate to struggles that a reader may be going through. The author's goal is to make sure the reader who is struggling to lose weight is inspired by reading this book and will make a lifestyle change. I, Amanda Lynn Wesley, created this book from the deepest love of my heart and with the authenticity in what I believe in. My opinions are expressed from experiences that I have while losing weight and the knowledge I gained from daily research and past mistakes. The opinions that I have may not reflect the opinions of the sources I used to cite while writing. I used the sources to back up the material I have written. Please look for a professional or a physician for complete medical and fitness advice. I am simply an average person who has successfully had a dramatic weight loss and wants to share my story. Diet and exercise have helped me lose weight and keep the weight off but are not the only contributing factors. I, as the author have written repeatedly in my book to emphasize subjects *but not limited to* changing habits, being disciplined, and have persistence which helped aid my success in weight loss management. I want to thank the readers for their time and consideration upon reading my book. I hope you, as the reader, have learned several things and understand what it truly takes to achieve goals. I did not want to have only stats and numbers for you to read, I also want to help you become open-minded by changing current habits that possibly have hindered you from achieving your goals. **This book was written to inspire you as the reader.** My motto is: If I can do it then you can do it. *You have this!*

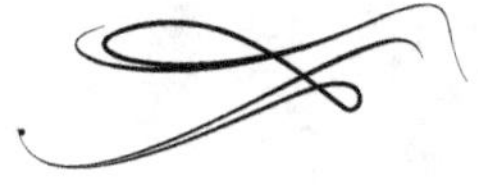

ABOUT THE AUTHOR

I am an avid runner and have completed numerous races, including national. I have finished first place in my gender/age category in one of the races I ran in 2022. I usually finish in the top 10-25% in the gender/age category. When I am not running, I enjoy boxing, yoga, swimming, weightlifting, rowing, and horseback riding. I pursue art and creativity when I am not exercising. I currently work as an administrative professional in healthcare and love helping people. I also love spending time with my friends, family, and my faith.